MW01245015

Blankets, Tea &
Crazy People

by

Sandra Heidi Anne

Wordclay
1663 Liberty Drive, Suite 200
Bloomington, IN 47403
www.wordclay.com

First published by Wordclay on 6/10/2008.

ISBN: 978-1-6048-1319-7 (sc)

Printed in the United States of America.

This book is printed on acid-free paper.

Contents

My Lover,
My Friend,
My Husband.
For making me feel brilliant,
I dedicate this book to you.

Prologue — Blankets, Tea & Crazy People

***Caution: Read with the understanding that this is
going to get intensely personal!***

I have always had a propensity towards getting urinary
tract infections, but after the birth of my second child, it
seemed I couldn't get rid of them. Returning to my OB/GYN
time after time with no results, he finally sent me to a well-
respected urologist at Vanderbilt Medical Center. After several
visits and different prescriptions, my symptoms were only
getting worse (this story is ultimately not about my bladder, I
am just giving a brief overview as a back-drop, if you will …
phew!). Not knowing quite what to do with me — and for
lack of a better category — I was diagnosed with *interstitial
cystitis*. To sum up … I was in chronic pain!

Mikey, my oldest son, was a colicky infant, screaming
through much of the day and night, sprinkled with intermittent
naps. This lasted till he was around eleven weeks old when
suddenly, to our great relief, he became the easiest and most
compliant child in existence. But something was triggered
in those post-delivery months. The drain of incessant pain
coupled with a screaming child brought on episodes where I

felt the sensation you get when you're about to take the first drop on a death-defying roller coaster. My heart would race within my breast and it felt as if my two-hundred-pound husband sat there. My skin would become cold and clammy and sometimes I would visibly shake. It was 1994 and this is how it all started.

I sat in the comfy recliner in my in-law's historic home near the French Quarter of New Orleans. My dear mother-in-law sat opposite of me with a look of concern. She asked if I would like a blanket and a cup of tea. I was having one of my attacks and she was hovering, longing to be useful. Actually, it was an inspired question. A soft cozy blanket to wrap around my tension riddled body and a cup of chamomile tea with a touch of honey would certainly do the trick! She quickly fetched both, and I hunkered down and attempted to breathe deeply.

Fast-forward three years...

I was buried in blankets and the anxiety attacks had degenerated to full-blown panic attacks and depression was nipping at my heels. One more child had been added to the family, but I was useless to my 8-month old because I lay in my bed unable to get up. All my muscles and bones were sound but the organ of my mind was not responding.

"I can't, I can't," circled my brain, like a snowball rolling downhill getting larger and heavier, gaining momentum with each rotation. I started to cry aloud inconsolably. Michael rushed in and tried to reason with me, but the ball seemed unstoppable. All I could do was repeat the mantra, "I can't…I can't…I can't."

Fifteen more months and after the birth of child number four…

It was dinnertime and Michael was working that evening. I was weak and trembling. The past few years had taken their toll and my mind was a fog. The kids were hungry.

"What's for dinner?" they chimed.

What's for dinner? A simple enough question…but I couldn't find an answer. *What's for dinner?* It echoed, though the children had all scurried away.

Think, Heidi…think! I can't! I can't! I can't! I just stood there…frozen. Trembling turned into shaking and tears streamed down my eyes, though I made no sound. I was under 100 pounds and in a round about way, was trying to kill myself through starvation. I returned to Vanderbilt again only this time to be checked into the psychiatric ward.

Today, June 1ˢᵗ, 2006

This book is an indirect chronicle of my healing. A testimony of deliverance…packed into epiphanies and ponderings. I am now — after extensive therapy, drugs, prayer and significant environmental changes — medication free and of a sound mind. For almost six years my life regularly descended into the pit of hell and my marriage almost collapsed under the flames. But God's mercy brought me out of the horrible pit and set me on a high place. He gave me a hope and a future. I cannot over stress this point… *this book is not meant to be read as doctrine or theology.* It is meant to be savored with a wide-open heart, rejoicing in how God can reveal the depth of His love in *all* ways and through *all* things.

As I put this together, I see my spiritual pilgrimage from my simplistic first entry, written at a time when I questioned the very character of God, to a faith that has been *refined by fire and proved genuine, resulting in Jesus Christ being revealed in glory* (1 Peter 1:7). That is why I have done my best, as my memory has allowed, to arrange the chapters in chronological order, so you also can grow with me.

Coupled with each chapter is a page from my "other" journals. The one's with no other purpose than to vent my feelings — a raw crying out. These are not in any order. It is my sincere desire that as you read both journals side-by-side, you will be encouraged and have an "emotional measuring stick," to view more clearly how deep the pit was and how great is our God.

Jesus came to me at the mall. He came to me in a child's animated movie. He came to me at a bed & breakfast. He came to me in a husband's stubborn love. He came to me through my children's eyes. He came to me in a thousand silly ways. He came to me in polar-fleece blankets and chamomile tea.

The Spirit of the Lord is on me,
Because he has anointed me
To preach good news to the poor.
He has sent me to proclaim freedom for
The prisoners and recovery of sight for the blind,
To release the oppressed, to proclaim
The year of the Lord's favor.

Luke 4:18 & 19

December 18, 1998

I feel as is if the Christianity I have been surrounded with my whole life has let me down. Nothing is fool proof. Nothing is black and white. Every answer ends with ten questions and it goes on and on. I am endlessly wandering — searching for this "elusive" truth — hoping for some happy ending. I don't want my life story to read "Memoirs of a Wretched Woman." I grow wearier and wearier of the battle. I feel as if hammers pound my head daily. How can this be? I have lived my whole life as the "good girl" always trying to do the right thing — always searching for truth so I could follow it. Always fearing I don't know enough — do enough. Where is the freedom? Where is the deliverance? Or is there no such thing? I know God has not promised us a life untouched by sin, but surely we are not left to the tormenting — or maybe this is hell. Jesus, Jesus, Jesus...I call on Your name. I can't see You. I can't feel You. I can't touch You — but You must be there. I'm drowning. I perish. Make Yourself real to me. I can never accept anything less than that.

Heidi

Bodacious Beds

There are times in life when a grateful heart comes easy. Praise and songs of thanksgiving seem to uncontrollably bubble to the forefront of everything I say and do. *This* is not one of those times! I will spare you the less than gory details that have led me to the pit that I find myself wallowing in. As I sit in the muck of self-pity, it occurs to me that maybe I should write in this journal. Because, unlike my other journals, where I dump all my vile and "vomitous" verbiage that no person should ever admit to, this journal is dedicated to higher ground; committed to thinking positive thoughts and hopefully, elevating me from my natural propensity towards the negative. My wise mother repetitively taught me that I could always find *something* to be thankful for if I set my mind to it. In my current hateful state, this does prove challenging. *But wait!* The path towards thankfulness is no further than the end of my toes. My BED!

My bed is a wonderful subject of loveliness! It has not always been so. Like many parents, I too used to neglect my own person in lieu of providing for others. It is not uncommon for the master bedroom in a house full of children to be the last one attended to. I decided a few years ago that I had had enough! I gathered up all the "unwantables" around the house and prepared for a "doosy" of a garage sale. I predetermined that all of the proceeds would go towards making our bedroom a haven and retreat. It was a booming success and sent me greedily on my way to the nearest department store.

There is no doubt in my mind that the focal point of every bedroom should be the bed! Our place of slumber should be like a glorious dream. You know the ones I'm referring to. They are flaunted on the cover of magazines and displayed in model homes. Beds that loft to the heavens with pillows stacked unto eternity. I can't help feeling the compulsion to run and throw myself in the center of the cloud and just float away. I was a woman on a quest! I bought feathers beneath and down above! Sheets, shams, duvet, you name it and I got it, all in tranquil tones of cream and caramel.

I don't remember my exact reaction the first evening I slept in my new sanctuary, but I can say still to this day, I love the way it feels to slip into my cushy marshmallow every night. My bed literally envelops me with a hug, comforting me after a hard day. Whenever I travel and eventually make it home to my bed I am brought to a new awareness of how much I am enchanted by it and have missed its sympathy. A strange love affair, I know, but as I seek refuge today and struggle with the ups and downs of hormonal imbalances, I curl way down deep, embraced on every side and my frown is turned upside-down.

Finally, brothers, whatever is true, whatever is noble, Whatever is right, whatever is pure, whatever is lovely, Whatever is admirable—if anything is excellent or Praiseworthy—thing about such things.

Philippians 4:8

Lord, once again I come before You aching with a pit in my stomach — and nausea. I don't know how to be free from this pain. It is amazing to me how I can go in to worship You with every intent to glorify You — draw near to You — know You more; then leave feeling like death and despair. The sin in my heart buries me. I have no purpose — I have no calling — or the calling I have is not the one I envisioned; to be a homemaker and raise two children, by myself. I feel You saying to me, "This is it. You will never achieve much significance in the world's eyes, but You will be great in My kingdom." My destiny is to always be in the shadow. If I were Godly and pure, I wouldn't care. I would be content to be a nobody. Why does it matter so much to me? Why am I torn in two? When I try to be a leader even in the tiniest ways — like Vacation Bible School — I'm told instead of teaching, I'll be organizing snacks ... augh! I am finding so much pride in my heart. I wonder if every "call" I thought I had on my life wasn't just a desire for self-glorification? I want to be freed of this pain and yet I keep hanging on — fearful that if I let go — I will disappear. My heart's desires and passions are obviously idolatry. Why am I dealing with this now? I thought all this jealousy and bitterness toward Michael was healed years ago. Help me Jesus. Give me the strength to lay down my cherished dreams — to sacrifice them on Your altar — to be obedient — and thankful — and fulfilled in what You have given me. Change my heart to see the value in whatever it is I am supposed to do with my life. Forgive me of my pride and need for self-exaltation. I confess that this is keeping me from being the kind of wife and mother and daughter of You that I need to be.

Heidi

Laying Lives Down

A few weeks ago I had the opportunity to sing at the church I grew up attending. There were still a few recognizable faces. Dear Mr. Holland, our personal *candy man* and distributor of monstrous gumballs to all the children after church, was there. I can count on one hand, in fact, one finger, how many sermons I remember, but I sure can recall anxiously awaiting closing prayer. As soon as the "Amen" was said, my brother and I would eagerly dash into the parking lot to take our place in line outside his familiar station wagon, for one of those rainbow-colored confections. The delight these little spheres produced among the youth of our church was incomparable, though short lived — losing their flavor within minutes after entering our cavity-filled mouths.

My eyes continued perusing the congregation for anything or anyone familiar, when they came to rest upon a girl and an aged woman. The girl, who I call a girl only because of her frail and child-like appearance, must have been in her late thirties, possibly forties, by now. Not knowing their names, their faces and figures registered with perfect clarity. The daughter still sat in her wheelchair seemingly unaware of her surroundings. I wondered at her specific disability. My uneducated guess would be a severe case of Down's Syndrome. As a child, fear would cause me to scurry and hide whenever I saw them at potlucks and socials, finding refuge behind my mother's skirts. To my immature mind she was disfigured, alien, frightening. And I ran, as I ran from all things uncomfortable.

Neither of them had changed, at least from an external perspective. After twenty-five years they seemed suspended in time. The dress and hairstyle unaltered from when I used to stare at a distance with morbid curiosity. Pale and sickly, the sight still made me squirm in my seat and I was overcome with thankfulness that all four of my children were "normal."

Drifting in my imagination, I pondered what life must be like for this dear mother who has never relinquished the most elemental responsibilities of caretaking … bathing, feeding, dressing her child. She has and will carry out those duties for the rest of her life. What an incredible task! The monotony of it all! Had there been any real tangible rewards for this mother? What has she received from all her labors? Has she ever shaken her fists at God and said *why me?* How many times has she wanted to quit, escape, run and never look back? Maybe not — maybe she is an emotionally and spiritually superior person who has never struggled in this way. I feel sure, in the same situation, I would have wrestled with God many a long and lonely night. Not only would I have shaken my fists, more than likely, I would have thrust them through a wall.

Right now I am raising four children ages 8, 5, 2 and 11 months — exhausted and living for the day when they are all in school and a little more self-sufficient. What if one of my children had been born with a disability? What if I had to walk a mile in her shoes? Round and round my mind labored, attempting to sort through painful self-evaluation, judgment, admiration, yearning. Not being able to come to any resolve, a thought broke through … *they are still here.* They are *still* here!

Still rolling into church just as they did twenty-five years ago. *Still* hanging on even when circumstances have not changed.

There has been no miraculous healing for them and yet they *still* cling to the promise of a savior. A savior Who is no stranger to suffering. A savior Who admonishes us to live nobly and with purpose. I would venture to believe that this woman has a depth of understanding into God's immeasurable love that few of us (me included) will ever acquire this side of heaven. I never really *knew* them — not then and not now — but I can learn. Embodied in our brothers and sisters all around us, if we will choose to see with our eyes and hear with our ears, we see the commandment of love fulfilled.

As the Father has loved Me, so have I loved you.
Now remain in My love.
If you obey My commands you will remain in My love,
Just as I have obeyed My Father's commands
And remain in His love.
I have told you this so that My joy may be in you
And your joy may be complete.
My command is this: Love each other as I have loved you.
Greater love has no one than this,
That he lay down his life for his friends.

John 15: 9-13

October 31, 2001

I am alone. There are people around me but still — I am alone. It is not my heart that hurts. It is deeper, or should I say, more centered. It is not a sharp pain — it is more like a squeeze that is so tight it cuts off every other sensation. If it were a tumor, I would make an incision right under my breast — in the middle — and take it out. But I know when I got inside, there would be nothing — just a hole that goes on for eternity. The question that haunts me — torments me — is "Why?" Why should someone with my life have such a vast nothingness inside? I try to come up with some pathetic justification ... my husband travels ... I have four children ... I can't keep my house clean ... I'm in pain with a disease. But when I objectively look at my life, I am deafened by my own inner judge. She has overwhelming evidence to support a case for a happy life. Therefore I must conclude that I am a bad person — a defective human being. In one sense it would be comforting if I didn't love You (Lord). At least then I could be categorized as "worldly." I wouldn't care about You, and could fill my cup with worldly pleasures. How did I get so @$&#!d up? How could I be taught about You my whole life — read Your Holy Bible — pray to You — hunger and thirst after righteousness — sacrifice personal wants and desires — learn my memory verses faithfully — not just follow the rules, but earnestly and emotionally love You. How does a person like that end up hopeless, fearful, irrational, psychotic, suicidal, lonely and desperate? What happened here? Where is the good news? How am I better off than an atheist? In fact, the atheist is better off because he is not continually tormented by a spiritual judge. Will this darkness ever lift? What good are all my blessings if I cannot enjoy them?

Heidi

Fabulous Fall

Lovely! Lovely! Whatever is *lovely*. If anything is excellent or praiseworthy, think on these things. I am on the way to our local YMCA to play some tennis and once again I am enraptured with the beauty that surrounds me, particularly at this time of year. The fall has for a long time been my favorite season. It seems to embrace whatever is warm and toasty in life. It throws me into a welcome reminiscence...

Cool days and even cooler nights ... the aroma of fireplaces permeating the neighborhood ... my family is huddled around a television with a long, pokey antennae, watching with both a fury and passion the Dallas Cowboys battle their arch enemies, the Washington Redskins on one of only four channels we received. Friday nights when my mother would bring a piping hot towel just from the dryer to wrap my chilled and freshly bathed body... turtleneck sweaters and raking leaves ... Halloween and the uncontainable rapture that explodes from a child when a holiday involves dressing up as a princess and gorging yourself on Milk Duds.

As I linger in the blissful complacency of my memories, I am arrested by the glory of my present surroundings, and the crown of all autumn delights — the *colors*! It seems a disservice to call them merely green, gold and red. Garnet, jade and flaxen *might* do. There are some occasions in life where language limits expression. As I view the rolling hills around me in Nashville, TN., I am in awe of their Creator.

There is, I am sorry to say, some scientific explanation for how each tree, each leaf in fact, seems to burst forth into joyous hues. But deep down in my child-self, where fancy and mystery are still allowed, I imagine billions of *Monet-like* fairies coming alive. Merrily working through each October night creating and revising each leaf into a completely unique masterpiece! Ooh! Here's another idea...mischievous elves hopping, hiding behind every leaf with an itty-bitty paintball gun; sticking out their miniscule insect-tongues as the paint explodes onto the foliage fortresses.

And still the *wonder* of God — far beyond myth or imagination! My whole being swells and then spills over into a river of joy! JOY! That I have eyes to see! JOY! That the world is not black and white! JOY! That I live in a place where I can experience the aesthetic beauty of the seasons! I am bemused when I consider the beginning of time on our planet earth. God looked out over all He had fashioned and said something like, "AWESOME," in our current vernacular. Can you not hear the glee in His voice? Can you not visualize the spectacular grin on His face? As I look around me on this crisp October day, I think the trees must be giving Him, the ultimate designer, a well-deserved standing ovation!

Great are the works of the Lord;
They are pondered by all
Who delight in them.

Psalms 111:2

July 10, 1999

Why do feelings have to play such a huge role in my life? Why do I have two people that live in my brain — arguing constantly? Somebody hear me! I'm sick! Somebody take care of me! I need help. I'm scared. I'm hanging on. What if I fall? I have to hang on — I have no choice. Sometimes I feel it would be nice to let go. I am so tired! Why do I feel that everyone's life would fall apart without me? Why am I scared that their lives wouldn't fall apart without me? I can't seem to make a decision. Do I go to church tomorrow or not? Do I spend the day at Nani and Bumpa's? I want to talk to someone and yet I'm tired of hearing myself complain. I keep trying to fill my days with things to distract me from my pain. My hope is gone and yet it isn't because I'm still here. Why can't you be a little more tangible God? Lord Jesus come back and take us home with You. Heal me — make me perfect — make me new. Take me out of this world. Help me while I'm here. Give me fresh revelation of purpose. Give me some sense that there is a reason for being here — that I have some significance to add. I feel as if all I am doing is draining everyone around me.

Heidi

Jesus Loves Me?

There are those fortunate people who go through life with a solid, experiential understanding of God's love for them – one, being my elder sister. Sometimes I listen with covetous awe as she describes how even as a child she felt like the apple of God's eye…Daddy's favorite! I, on the other hand, think that the below-mentioned, universal, multi-generational childhood tune expresses my take on God's love. Let's refresh ourselves …

> Jesus loves me this I know
> For **the Bible tells me so**. (you know how it goes)
> Chorus
> Yes, Jesus loves me.
> Yes, Jesus loves me.
> Yes, Jesus loves me.
> **The Bible tells me so**.

A choice — an intellectual ascension — to believe that Jesus does love me for the Bible *tells* me so, and not because I necessarily *feel* that it is so.

In the quiet moments of youth when I was stilled from all my busyness — my trying to impress God with what a good little girl I was — there was a fear, no, a *terror,* that gripped me. A deep sense that I wasn't invited to the party. That somehow no matter how hard I tried I would still end up with my nose pressed against the window, looking in at all the party hats, wishing I too could come in.

Picture with me the scene — Noah's Ark. There I am. The giant door is shut. The rain comes down first as a drizzle, then a downpour. Panicked crowds rush the monstrous ship — banging, pleading — between gulps of water and gasps for air. Perishing with them, I pound the door.

"Please, oh please let me come in!" Whatever God was offering, I was terrified that somehow I would miss it. The fine print would get me in the end and it would be too late. With this little insight into my childhood psyche, now fast forward to adulthood.

Yesterday God graciously sent a rainbow, a sign of remembrance, to illuminate the unstable atmosphere of my soul. It was Sunday and Michael was gone, as usual. Timmy woke me up at five o'clock after an already miserable and restless night. All I wanted to do was to pull the covers over my head.

"Forget church!" I addressed the empty bedroom. "I just don't have the energy to do it!"

For those of you who have children, you understand the stamina and efficiency it takes to get four children and yourself dressed into your Sunday best, fed and in the pews by 8:30 am. For those of you who don't, no disrespect, but you're just clueless.

When I had reconciled myself to the idea that it was absolutely, positively physically and emotionally impossible to pull it together — miraculously, like an *I Dream of Jeannie* bob of the head — we were there. Maybe not in our Sunday best and a little rough around the edges, but just the same, we were there.

Sandwiched in between my offspring, singing songs of praise...BAM! It hit me. An unsolicited mental movie began to play in the theatre of my mind. Two heavenly angels — looking very much like the ridiculous cliché we mortals have made them, complete with white cotton robes, bleached-blonde hair and chicken-feather wings protruding from their shoulder-blades — were perched above me. They had the most brilliant expression on their faces. The topic of conversation was to my delight...me.

"She did it!" said the first one warmly. *"It was a tough battle this morning, but she fought through. Doesn't she look great?"*

"Yeah, she does and look at the kids...there is nothing quite like little children singing. It just makes me tingly all over. She really loves her kids. I'm so proud of her!" Chimed Angel II.

My matinee may seem trivial and silly, after all, it's not as if I'd healed the sick or anything. And come to think of it, it didn't even directly involve God but his messengers. The impact? I choked back the tears. It's amazing how easy it is to entertain voices of criticism and accusation. But praise I hold at a skeptical distance. For a few moments I *felt* precious. For a few moments I *felt* loved. For a few moments I wore my sisters shoes. Could it be that I was significant enough that heavenly beings would care to notice anything I did? Too soon the moment was gone. Fleeting and delicious, like a whiff of some exotic perfume, it filled my senses briefly and I knew the source.

How I long to bathe in that perfume; to soak in its spices until I'm all "pruney." Here's a lofty goal...to be so literally drenched in the love of God that it oozes from my every pore. To smell so *love*-ly, that when I pass by, others would stop dead in their tracks just to breathe deeply. And just maybe, then I could help someone else move from being a pressed nose up against a window pane, to experiencing life on the inside — warm, safe and secure.

I pray that you, being rooted and established in love,
May have power, together with all the saints,
To grasp how wide and long and high
and deep is the love of Christ,
And to know this love that surpasses knowledge—
That you may be filled
To the measure of all the fullness of God.

Ephesians 3:17-19

1999

    My hole is dark and deep — with scary things all around. I spend my days trying to find holds to pull myself out. I stretch — I climb — but never make it to the top. Sometimes my Lover comes and pulls me out. He throws a rope down and today I have the strength to climb. But other days my strength is gone. He may call to me and throw the rope — but I have no hope. I don't want to go out into the sunshine because when I'm put back in the hole it takes too long for my eyes to adjust to the dark. I cry out to my Lover, sometimes loud, sometimes inaudibly. Get me out! Do whatever it takes — just get me out! Don't leave me alone in my hole. Sometimes I know He is there and He is willing. Other times I know He is there — I hear him — but He has no ears. I get angry. I get sad. After all, His arms must get tired. What lover wants a "hole person" – dirty, heavy, dark? I become one with the darkness and disappear. Where is my Lover? Where is my light?

Heidi

Friday the 13th

Friday the 13th. As a rational adult and a Christian I know I am not supposed to be superstitious, but I have to admit that sometimes there seems to be a strange order at work. Have you ever noticed that as you are basking in the joy of marital bliss and happen to comment to your spouse, "Dear, how *deliciously* you and I are getting along," before nightfall World War III has descended upon you? Or maybe you are cruising the highway praising God for how well your car has held up, right before the engine falls out. I'm not sure exactly how all of this fits into my story other than sometimes I get a little frightened when I start getting thankful out loud.

There is a young girl sitting in the driver's seat of a smashed up car and she will probably never pass another Friday the 13th again without a cold chill going down her spine. My husband and I were taking some time to invest in our relationship. After a lovely Italian lunch, we toyed with the idea of catching a movie. Nothing tempted us, so we aimlessly drove the streets until we happened upon the scene of an accident at a busy four-way intersection.

Now, if you've ever been in a car wreck it will forever haunt you. I thought back to my accident. How sudden! How shocking! One minute you are singing *Zip-ah-dee-doo-dah* with your kids, the next an airbag slams into your chin! Screeching brakes! Crushing metal! Children screaming! Bodies shaking! What a horrifying experience!

There she was with her door all crunched in and I thought to myself what a miracle it was that she was seemingly uninjured. There was an older woman, standing at her side, consoling her as the policeman approached. She was crying. Was it her parent's car, I thought? Was she terrified of their reaction? More than likely she was barely recovering from the shock and bewilderment.

As I sat viewing the drama unfold, a stream of thoughts flowed from my subconscious flooding my reality. I could be gone in an instant. Life is so fragile. I am completely out of control. Scary! It has always been my understanding that meditating on truth is beneficial and that by so doing, the truth will set you free.

One slice of truth is this … much of our lives *are* completely out of our control. Life is like a match that is lit and gone. Hopefully coming into contact with the disturbing fact of our own mortality will scare us into really living: to forgive quicker and make the first step toward reconciliation, to build a fort with our kids right in the middle of the family room, to dance in the rain with our lover, to chew our food well and delight in letting the flavors ride the wave of digestion over titillated taste buds, to be overwhelmed by a sunset, or better yet a sunrise!

I am thankful that we have these large and small reminders that we are not gods and have a limited time and space to work with. I am thankful that this particular reminder passed without any permanent damage to anyone. I am also overwhelmingly thankful that it isn't me sitting on the other side of that smashed-in door, but can ponder these things through the benefit of observation.

Show me, O Lord, my life's end
Let me know how fleeting is my life.
You have made my days a mere handbreadth;
The span of my years is as nothing before You.
Each man's life is but a breath.

Psalms 39:4&5

September 2001

    Pain, pain — deep and aching. Nothing shows on the outside. The hole inside of me seems endless. My body is a colander — no matter what is poured into me — it just flows right out. Pain, pain — twisted and twisted. Love me — please love me! You say you do, but I can't feel it — make me feel it. Love me enough to love me hard! You keep stepping back — or maybe I push You. Either way it is harder for me to feel You. There is too much distance between us. Clothe me — cover me — take care of me. I feel naked even when I can see the clothes on my body. Don't break me. I'm scared. You hold me in Your hands. You think I am made of vinyl — but I am not! I am porcelain. If You drop me I will shatter into a million pieces. Please don't break me. Hold me, touch me, play with me, think that I am beautiful. Put me on display and admire me — a fine porcelain doll. Please be careful — this is who I am.

Heidi

Tubby Troubles

I am a bit embarrassed to admit the cause of my thankful heart today. Shallow and vain, I reveal my truly adolescent spiritual age. In a time when everyone is afraid to speak plainly for fear of being labeled intolerant, and we walk on the proverbial eggshells continuously, I am going to throw falsehood to the wind and proclaim, "I am thankful I am not fat!" As impolitic as it is to say, it is no less true.

Today as I was eating at the mall with my husband and two little ones, my husband brought my attention to an extremely obese woman nearby. I am not proud of the fact that we were gawking at someone so unfortunate, but it was difficult not to look! I don't think, ever in my life, I have seen someone *that* fat in person. I do not say this for humor's sake when I tell you that I am positive that one or two more pounds would keep her entirely confined to a bed.

Here I am at home, thinking about her, wondering. The emotional and physical agonies she must suffer! I remember each of my pregnancies. I was definitely not glowing! All the added weight made me miserable — the aches — the pains! Struggling with simple tasks, like climbing a flight of stairs, turning over in bed or tying my shoes. I recall the first time I could jump and run after giving birth to my daughter. You would have thought I had been crippled. I leapt for joy — giddy!

As if all the physical challenges wouldn't be enough, to feel the stares of disapproval and pity wherever you go — or far worse to be mocked! Let us not forget the brutal honesty of children. Inexperienced in the ways of social graces, I believe each of my four children at one time blurted out some humiliating remark resembling, "She's got a BIG bottom Mommy!" These comments are made rather innocently and not intended for harm, but what about children a little older, who for more sinister reasons purposefully taunt obesity?

Think also about the practical challenges. Having to wait longer than anyone else at a restaurant because you *required* a booth, being unable to fit in a normal size chair, getting an airline ticket — would you have to buy two? How about the mortification of going into a plus-size store only to find that nothing fits — the horror!

I am reminded of a movie I saw years ago starring Johnny Depp and Leo DeCaprio called *What's Eating Gilbert Grape*. Though the plot of this overcast drama did not directly deal with excessive weight gain, through Gilbert, his obese mother and mentally challenged younger brother, we can vicariously and uncomfortably live out the struggles of being a social misfit. Movies can be helpful in that way. They can help us to gain some perspective or insight into things that otherwise are unfamiliar to us. And I am unfamiliar with an overload of fat.

Don't hate me because I am thin (at least for now anyway). There was a short period in college when I struggled with my weight. In retrospect, the fact that I "struggled" at all was strictly self-imposed considering I am 5'6" tall and never weighed more than 130 lbs. After birthing four children I have an unusually slim figure, weighing in at about 110 lbs. People, particularly women, are forever commenting on my size.

"How do you do it?" They ask.

"I don't believe you ... did you adopt?"

This attention makes me uncomfortable. I'm never really sure how to respond. It's not as if I have *done* anything. I deserve no praise or applause. Ever since I turned twenty, I have been free to eat whatever I want without much effect. My metabolism is what it is. I'm not boasting. That would be as ridiculous as bragging about the size of my feet. By all accounts I *should* have a weight problem ... I LOVE FOOD! Anyone that claims an intimate acquaintance with me, knows that life's events are remembered by the dishes served — food is love!

Each of my anniversaries are filed and recorded in my mind according to dessert, entrée and atmosphere — in that order. Also, being a fairly undisciplined person, these mainstay qualities — preoccupation with food and a decidedly low will power — could have been disastrous for someone with a different genetic map.

Why? Why was I designed this way? Why do some people deprive themselves, sweat bullets and still gain five pounds from just looking at a Krispy Kreme doughnut? I don't know the answers to such silly questions. I don't know the answers to many more questions with far more gravity. I can't resolve it — so I'll just be thankful.

> For you created my inmost being.
> You knit me together in my mother's womb.
> I praise You because I am fearfully and wonderfully made.
>
> Psalm 139: 13 & 14

July 2000

It is a typical day where I am unaware of the actual date. In fact, nothing seems to exist outside of these four walls. My inability to complete a "to do" list remains a mystery. My back is aching. My feet are aching. I have been up and running since 5:30 this morning — it is 7:35 in the evening and I have just put the children to bed. As usual, I lost my temper over some little thing. The baby is screaming and I just want to scream at someone! The house is an utter disaster! And I am so angry!! I hate Michael for leaving me! I hate him for every time I leave him with the kids and come back to a straightened house! I hate my mother-in-law for the same reason! I hate Michael for being better than me at music! I hate Michael for being better than me at everything! How can I ever get this hate out of my heart? How can I ever get rid of this pain and anger? I hate myself for being mediocre at everything I do! I hate that I can never seem to keep a clean house! I am miserable! I am drowning! Michael and I have never been on such bad terms. I am a wreck! I would rather disappear than live the rest of my life like this. There is no way out. There is no way out. There is no way out.

Heidi

Music City Miracle

It was a cool, overcast April morning. I picked up my father in-law and we were on our way to the Nashville *Music City Marathon*. My dear mother-in-law at age sixty-three had decided to take up power-walking…GO MOM! With little inconvenience, we found a parking place and followed the signs and people who seemed to know where they were going. We had agreed the rendezvous would be at the finish line. Having never been to a marathon, my senses were overly stimulated by brightly colored banners and sounds blasting from nearby loud speakers. Toss in the heady smell of diesel fuel, mingled with what might have been funnel cakes, and you can appreciate the fact that I was enjoying a truly distinctive experience.

The crowd was moderate when we arrived, but shortly thereafter, excited family members and friends, holding signs and pom-poms, were packed in from all vantage points. Peering, squinting, standing on tip-toe — anxious for the first glimpse of their loved ones coming down the home stretch. Typically, I might be described as an empathic person, so it is not strange that I found myself "osmotically" transported into the lives of perfect strangers around me.

First in view, were the isolated mega-athletes — characterized by the *been-here-done-it-a-zillion-times* look on their faces. Not to mention, appearing so relaxed and refreshed, you would think they were just starting the twenty-six mile journey rather than making the last turn. They were the pro's, running in time with some super-human inner rhythm.

After a healthy pause — the bell-curve arrived. Some runners were coupled, hand-in-hand. I can only speculate that there must have been moments when one gave the other the courage to go on, possibly to stop and rub a cramped muscle if need be. Others ran as a team; decked out in color-coordinated t-shirts and full of spirit! As soon as one would cross the finish line he or she would make a straight path into the crowd to cheer on their other teammates, barely even stopping to glory in *their* moment. Some participants were handicapped and finished proudly on wheels, their veins bulging from over-taxed arms.

Time marched on and others trickled in one by one — wracked in pain, faces grimaced, contorted and hobbling with sweat and tears pouring from their bodies. *Pay attention, this is where it gets really good.* The crowd in unrehearsed unity began to swell in assistance for these brave souls — willing them to fight! My voice joined in the bracing chorus — whooping and hollering! I was touched deeply by the strength of mind, body and spirit it must take to accomplish such a daunting task.

I have always been fascinated and inspired when I see someone set a goal, make the necessary sacrifices, discipline themselves and endure unto the achievement of that goal. The life lessons one can extrapolate from this scene are numerous. But what struck me the most is how at the finish line of a marathon, people really seem to *"get it."*

Generally speaking, in life, it is first to break the ribbon that receives the accolades. You know … the beautiful people, the movie star, the homecoming queen, the most valuable player. They are the ones that get lifted onto the shoulders of their teammates and are paraded around like heroes. We scream for rock stars, chanting their names. We line up along the red carpets for a glimpse of an idol, casting rose petals at their feet to tread upon. We elevate the biggest, the brilliant and the best!

But *here,* on the last stretch of pavement, it was conclusive. The weariest traveler, the struggler, the weakest link, the least likely to succeed, the one that at any moment might give it all up and collapse from pain and fatigue — these were the ones that compelled the crowd. Voices singularly pierced through the throng, crying out … *You can do it! You've got it! … We believe in you! … Just a little further, don't stop now! … I'm so proud of you! … I love you!* Even now I still get choked up thinking about it.

There was absolutely zero percent chance of holding back the tears. And in that moment I prayed, "God, help me to look for the way-worn traveler today. Open my eyes to discern which of my friends or family are entertaining despair. Help me to come along beside them. To empower weary arms, legs and spirits. Help me to help them on toward the finish line."

The body is a unit, though it is made up of many parts;
And though all its parts are many, they form one body.
So it is with Christ. For we were all baptized by
One Spirit into one body.
Those parts of the body that seem to
be weaker are indispensable,
And the parts that we think are less honorable
We treat with special honor.
And the parts that are unpresentable are treated with
Special modesty, while our presentable
parts need no special treatment.
But God has combined the members
of the body and has given
Greater honor to the parts that lacked
it, so that there should be no
Division in the body, but that its parts
should have equal concern
For each other. If one part suffers,
every part suffers with it;
If one part is honored, every part rejoices with it.

I Corinthians 12: 12, 13 & 22-26

October 25, 2001

Michael and I received news this morning that David Coy suddenly passed away…died. What a tragedy! What grief I feel for this precious family! Why God, why? Of all the people in the world that should die — why didn't You intervene? Why did You spare his life a few months ago in that terrible crash, only to take it now? Wouldn't it have been easier on those poor children had he gone then? Oh, the overwhelming and choking sadness! How will they ever come through this trial? Oh, how I wish I had a more stable theology to fall on Lord. The only thing that comforts me is to believe that You are crying too. What does it mean that You'll never give us more than we can bear? I don't know if the world is so much worse now or if I'm just so much more aware of what is going on. I have lived a very sheltered life up until these last few years. What a year of death and tragedy this has been. How I long for some understanding! How I long for some comfort! You seem so very far from me and I feel like I live in poverty. I may have nice clothes but I am naked. My eyes may see but I am blind. Have mercy on me. Of all the people in the world why would You listen to me? I am a wretch! I have everything I need and still I am thankless and miserable. I have so much and I wallow in self-pity. Where is the Holy Spirit's work in my heart? How could I be saved and be full of such evil? Forgive me Lord! Help me to be this "light" that Your word talks about. I feel as if I have nothing to give anyone but tears. Help me to teach my children about You. Help me to love You. I am so terribly lost and alone. Hold me together.

Heidi

Kissing Boo Boos

"Dad!" My son hollered. "Nanie's on the phone and says it's important!"

My husband and I were lazily cuddling in bed — ignoring the inevitable. The sun had been calling to us far too long and now, our literal son was calling. Michael picked up the phone on our bedside table and I could tell by the immediate wrinkling of his brow that something was wrong. I propped my head on his chest hoping to glean some information from his responses. It wasn't working. Somehow I instinctively knew this was *not* the time for me to do the usual butting in and forcing an unwanted three-way conversation. So, I anxiously awaited the dial tone. It came. Kaylee, Michael's niece and daughter of his only sister, was in the hospital with meningitis.

"Meningitis," I gasped!

Words like coma, seizure, brain damage and death ran across the billboard of my mind. *What kind of meningitis?* I wondered. With four children I had experienced enough "well-baby" visits to know that there were two strains of the disease — one being the more serious. Of course "well-baby" is just a code name to lull you into complacency, until you are no longer ignorant of the fact that what that *really* means is physically restraining your screaming child while they get inoculated for everything from measles to Himalayan spotted fever. Hold it! I'm getting side-tracked…back to Kaylee.

Isn't this one of the required shots? Had the vaccination not worked? I started frantically looking for my baby bible, <u>What</u>

to Expect the First Year. Having opened it up hundreds of times to the section on childhood illness, it fell right on the appropriate section. *Okay, there are two kinds, but they seem to have the same symptoms.* I mumbled to myself with concern.

As soon as I received the phone number for Miami Children's Hospital, I called my weary and burdened sister-in-law. Dana filled me in on the details, which were very few. Poor little Kaylee *had* tested positive but even the doctor's were unsure as to which strain and she had to remain in the hospital seven to ten days for observation. I could hear the agonizing fear and exhaustion in her voice. Doing my best to say the right words and attempt to be reassuring, I knew it just wasn't good enough.

"Dana, can I pray with you right now?"

This felt a little risky. My own relationship with God had not been that cozy in the past few years and I definitely did not have what I would call a spiritually dynamic relationship with my sister-in-law. Was I making her uncomfortable and causing her more stress? Would she be offended? I was relieved when she replied with a deep sigh of gratitude, "Yes!"

I began stumbling over my words – frustrated — I was definitely not in "the zone." I thought back to the time when I would have taken off on the prayer highway — map in hand — directions clear. The rebuking would commence, demons would be bound, power in the blood of the Lamb proclaimed. My tongue would seem to flow as if on autopilot. But after many unanswered prayers, and my faith left on the side as road kill, my talks with God had toned down recently.

Finally, after what seemed like a lot of mumbo-jumbo, I found the exact words I had been searching for. "Father, help us … make it better. Amen."

We hung up and I hoped somehow that she had been strengthened by my call. As I painstakingly rehearsed the conversation in my mind, making many sour judgments on myself, I was struck with the simple request that I had finally come to rest upon. It is an often used phrase in our home — *Mommy, kiss it and make it better.* Between my three active boys I have found it necessary to stockpile chapstick in response to the cracking that occurs from the continual kissing of boo-boos. They are in pain. They are frightened and the first thing they reach for is Mommy's touch — Mommy's kiss.

Although it may not immediately nor miraculously heal their wound, it is amazing how tender compassion and empathy soothes their sobbing bodies. Relaxing into understanding arms somehow acts as an effective anesthetic. Although I believe God *can* and *has* healed … what happens when He doesn't? All I can do is turn my face upward, stretch out my arms and in childlike faith say, "Daddy, kiss my boo-boo."

Do not be anxious about anything,
but in everything by prayer and petition,
with thanksgiving, present your requests to God,
and the peace of God which transcends all understanding
will guard your hearts and minds in Christ Jesus.

Philippians 4: 6 & 7

May 12, 2000

It is Saturday. Michael is gone. I have just sent Meghan and Mikey to their rooms. They are constantly bickering. Joseph has been whiney and needy since he woke up and the baby is particularly out of sorts. I couldn't sleep last night — my mind kept racing. I kept feeling a sense of panic. Like if things don't change very quickly — I'm going to blow a fuse. I love my children — I love my husband — but I feel completely lost! I feel such a deep, empty sadness. I feel no direction, no purpose for my life. Lost! Lost! Lost in my relationship with God — lonely and sad — lonelier than ever before. Is life supposed to be this way? I thought by now I'd have so much more figured out. To be a tormented soul and then become immortal is one thing. But to live this hell and then disappear as a vapor? Where is God? Where is love? I believe there is a creator who is God; the complexities of the universe and our world demand that this must be true. I believe that this God, out of love, became man and died for our sins. He took the penalty for our sins. Why do I believe this? I don't know... because not to believe would take everything I know as reality and dash me into nothingness. I must believe as I must have oxygen, and yet this belief and what it really means seems as unattainable as God himself. I find no answers that don't end with a question mark. I find no scripture that cannot be twisted and molded so each of us can erect our own statue of religion. I find no understanding. If one thing is untrue then how can I believe any of it? And so I crumble again — back down to this unshakeable thing in my gut! Maybe it is fear? Maybe it is brainwashing? Maybe it is faith — that beyond all explanation I do believe there is a God and Jesus lives!

Heidi

The Gospel According to Heidi

I have been a Christian as far back as my memory will carry me. There is a distinct picture in my mind of being in my bedroom in a house called "Epping." If you find it odd that I have a name for my house, let me elaborate. My parents were in real estate and we changed addresses the way most people change shoes. One advantage in our itinerant lifestyle is that I can very easily estimate my age. So, this particular house and this particular memory would put me at around five years old.

I had a little chart taped next to my door — nothing fancy — just a handwritten note on a plain white sheet of paper. On it were a few daily chores: brushing teeth, getting dressed and so forth. But what stands out in my memory was an assignment to memorize the Lord's Prayer. This, I did along with many other scriptures. What a blessing to be raised in a home where knowing the word of God was just as expected as putting on my underwear — just as essential as oral hygiene. God was the nose on the clock; life always going, moving, circling, but ever around Him.

So there it is — I am a Christian — and come from a strong Christian heritage. But don't be mislead; I am by nature a skeptic. When it comes to theology, in what I'll categorize as the "non-essentials," I have been all over the map trying to find a rest stop. My mind races with questions and with each answer more questions are birthed. At times I get so bogged down, so intellectually burdened, my brain gets a little sick. I have often joked (though it is not funny) that I don't ever have to get out of bed to be exhausted.

Praise the Lord for my husband! I am so grateful for him. He looks at the world and Word and takes it at face value. He has such a simple, peaceful faith, unlike me, searching for the hidden meanings and the deeper meanings underneath the hidden meanings and the buried meanings underneath those. He helps me to lasso my emotions and thought patterns when they are spinning out of control and pulls me back to the simple Gospel … Good News!

There was a time a couple of years ago when I found myself asking, "What is the Good News?" *There* is a strange thing for a seasoned Christian to ask. Allow me to clarify one more thing … I have never been one of those "unsaved Christians" that we talk about, meaning people who are around church stuff, but never really surrender to Jesus. I believe this point is crucial because I want you, the reader, to understand that you can be a very sincere and devout follower of our Lord and still pass through deep valleys of shadows and doubt. I tried to reject God. It seemed that if there *was* a God then he was most certainly *not* a *good* God. Or, if He *was* good then He was not omnipotent and was getting a sound spanking from the devil.

God is so merciful that He places boundaries around His children. I think of the time I had a vision of a gigantic hand, thirty times the size of myself, with the palm facing up and I am perched at the very tip of His middle finger looking down at the abyss. Leaning forward, I am convinced I'm going to fall, but something has me by the back of my overalls. I can't see it, but it is the other hand of God, protecting me from myself. It was during this dark time that God gave me a simple analogy that spoke deeply to my heart about His good news.

I now invite you into this unabashedly gut-wrenching, shamelessly emotionally driven drama. Starring the queen of hysteria ... Sally Fields (re: *Steel Magnolias* or *Not Without My Daughter*), or if you prefer a male, you could easily substitute Mel Gibson who has equal prowess in the "losing it" category.

She's behind the wheel driving to that all too familiar destination. Not able to eat that morning, her stomach souring at the thought of chemo, not for herself, but her eight year old son, Mikey. He would surely not be eating for several days.

"Will this ever end? How did this happen? Didn't I do everything a good mother should? I made him wear his coat in the winter chill; limited his intake of candy bars and soda pop. I tried to always ensure he had a good night sleep. Did I miss something? Why—Why—Why?"

This circled in her mind like a talking doll with a no off-button. Adjusting her mirror, she peaks at her son. His pink, squishy baby-fat cheeks, were now replaced with a transparent, skim milk-like covering. His cheekbones accentuated by sunken eyes with circles around circles. But all this would be nothing if he would just smile.

She remembered running her fingers through his thick chocolate brown hair and how she used to tackle his "Alfalfa-like" cowlick at the back of his head. No amount of gel could rob its independent spirit. What gel couldn't do — cancer did. Now he had a different baseball cap for everyday of the week. She found that this distraction took away the sting of being bald in the second grade. He had been poked and prodded so many times that now the crying fits and begging had subsided, leaving behind a courageous resolve — the kind that can only be gained through harsh reality; a reality that was never meant for him. He was born to laugh, to run, play baseball at the park with his friends, climb a tree and hang from its limbs. Now he contents himself with a good "spy" book and Legos.

They roll into the parking lot and gather their gear, never knowing if they may have to stay overnight. Once inside, the nurse brings her alone into the doctor's office, leaving Mikey behind engrossed in his latest Game Boy game. She is surprised at how quickly the doctor joins her.

After a few uncomfortable superficial exchanges he blurts out, "The cancer is advancing more rapidly than anyone had anticipated." She tries to calm the rising tide of terror. From that point on it is a blur. Cliché phrases like, "I'm sorry, there's nothing more we can do," are muffled in her mind, fighting through the barricade of denial. On the way home she is suspended in time, with all of her energies focused on one thing — *keep it together, keep it together*. Though the sky is blue she is in a fog.

The following days turn from gray and hopeless to black and haunting. The screams of agony from her son, are accompanied by a messenger from hell riding the ebony horse of death, with fire and stench in his nostrils. He mocks as he drags her treasure slowly into the pit. She takes a cool cloth to his head, wiping away the droplets of perspiration that had accumulated during the last wrenching episode. He looks into her bloodshot eyes as both their tears unite making the edge of his pillowcase soggy.

"*Help me,*" he says in a cracked whisper. "*Help me.*" He drifts into an exhausted slumber. Afraid to leave his side but unable to wrestle her emotions into submission another moment, she runs for the bedroom closet. Shoving a pillow over her face she screams. The walls of determined stoicism have been breached and the long repressed armies of anger, fear, love and helplessness storm her fortress. Violently shaking, she falls to the floor, her hands clasp her midsection tightly as she doubles over. A river of tears and mucus string from her chin. Not even bothering to wipe it away, out of the depths of the her soul comes a guttural wail… "OOOOHHH GAAAAHHHHHHHD!!!!! TAKE THIS FROM MY SON! PLEEAAASSEE GOD! I LOVE HIM!!! GIVE IT TO ME!!! *PLEASE…* GIVE IT TO ME!!!!

CUT

Now, picture with me, God looking to this earth. He sees the millions of hollow eyes. He sees children with no food in their bellies and no hope in their hearts. He sees fields soaked crimson with blood. He hears the dying soldier calling for his mommy. He sees people plummeting to their deaths from a burning tower. He watches a girl frantically scrub herself in the shower, weeping because she will never get clean from the violation of her body just hours earlier. He sees the rejected little boy in the corner of the cafeteria who thinks its better to be invisible than to be taunted. He sees *every* broken heart, *every* broken home, *every* broken life from the beginning of time to eternity, and with a sound that dwarfs the thunder he screams, "GIVE IT TO ME! TAKE THIS FROM MY CHILDREN AND GIVE IT TO ME."

That is exactly what he did … gave it to *Himself!*

Here is our condition — all of us — slowly making our way toward hell, and while I am not sure exactly what that is; if it is worse than the hell-on-earth that I have known (and it is), then horror is appropriate. He, Jesus, the Son of God, walked that path for us, but when *He* faced death and hell, the creator could never be subject to the created. The Ever Existing could not be bottled in time; instead He exploded back onto the scene that monumental Sunday morning with a message.

Believe in God … believe in Me. Life is going to get hard and you might be tempted to forget that I love you … but I love you. If you disobey Me … I love you. If you run away … I'll run after you. If you hit Me and yell at Me … I'll still love you and try to heal your anger. Hold on, believe that I love you and will come for you. I am coming to take you away from all this. You can't imagine, in your wildest dreams, what I am preparing for you. Time will pass and the world will try to say, "It never happened … I never happened." Don't believe it! Get still … get quiet … get away from all the noise. Look to the mountains, view the vastness of the skies, study the sunset, and you will remember Me.

You will hear My voice, not with your ears but from the inside out. I'll be calling to you … I love you … I love you!

And *that* my friends, is the GOOD NEWS!

For I am convinced that neither death nor life,
Neither angels nor demons,
Neither the present nor the future, nor any powers,
Neither height nor depth,
Nor anything else in all creation,
Will be able to separate us from the love of
God that is in Christ Jesus our Lord.

Romans 8:38&39

November 1, 2001

*What a busy and hectic week I am having … Halloween
parties, Mikey's birthday, our car breaking down.   I survived
through yesterday — that is good.   As I have glanced over this
journal, I have confirmed what I already knew.   I am having way
more than a few bad days!   I am disgusted with the fact that I
may have to go back on medication.   It is not so much "depression"
(yet anyway), more like severe anxiety.   I took the kids trick-or-
treating around our neighborhood last night and in the process
met two stay at home moms.   They both were so excited to meet
me and expressed their desire to connect and become friends.   Well
the very thought has put me into a panic this morning.   How
can I be a Christian?   I am certainly not a light to the world.
My life is completely overwhelming.   I absolutely laugh at the
state of my house.   I say laugh — but it deeply disturbs me.   I
simply cannot handle all of my responsibilities.   I am utterly
failing in every area of my life. I have been a miserable friend
to the few friends I have and now I have two neighbors wanting
to join the neglected few.   I wish Michael took them last night!
The assistant pastor spoke this last Sunday about coming into
church so filled up that you're ready to give.   I can't remember
the last time I was on anything but empty.   My life is like how
my parent's treat their cars … put in five-dollars and drive it
until at any moment you are out of gas and stranded on the side
of the road.   Pull into a station — two gallons — and you're off
— over and over again — never a filled tank.   It all makes me
question my salvation.   Michael is extremely stressed and moody
lately, which only compounds the problems.   I am starting to feel
hopeless.   Oh God, help me!   Change me!   I don't know how else
to pray.   I am a miserable wretch who cannot get her act together.*

Heidi

I Lose! I Lose!

You have heard it said over and again by parents' through out the ages: while they anticipated teaching their children, they were amazed at just how much their children have taught them. I am no exception.

It is dinnertime and as usual the O'Brien home is full of raucous play. Toddlers are running underfoot, filling their lungs to capacity and shouting every few minutes, "I'm hungry!" or, "Joseph pushed me!" In between the scuffles, the older children take turns inquiring about the evening menu. And I can guarantee that nine times out of ten, someone will respond with a look or grunt of disgust. Who was it that conceived the term "*Happy* Homemaker?" Trust me when I say, no one is knocking on my door asking me to be the poster child for *that* slogan.

The water begins to boil and I am involved in the intricate and highly complicated process of putting the rolls in the oven, cooking the pasta, chopping the veggies, washing the lettuce — which will all miraculously culminate into an sumptuous, nutritious and eye-pleasing culinary delight! Just as I am in the delicate and crucial maneuverings of achieving my goal — without setting off the fire alarm — all of the chaos underfoot makes a path to the very last nerve in my body. Thus, producing a tirade where I command the children to be scattered to the west winds of their rooms.

My tantrum is having less of an impact than desired, and I can only apply the adage *familiarity breeds contempt*. With my hands on my hips, stopping to assess the situation, I briskly ask, "What is going on here?"

Joseph whizzes by with Timmy nipping at his heels. For the moment, dinner takes its place on the back burner, and I am a spectator of the 15-meter dash. My two preschoolers race the track from our foyer, through the family room, kitchen and dining rooms, back to the foyer as quickly as their miniature legs can go. Joseph, the older of the two, is of course more adept at this and has just recently bought into the whole competitive thing. As they cross the imaginary finish line he gloats over his little brother, "I win! I win!"

Timmy, joyfully parrots him, "I win! I win!"

Incredulous, Joseph barks back "No you don't! You *lose*!"

Timmy stops a moment to assimilate the new information. Unaware of and immune to the shame, disappointment and horror of being labeled a loser, he hops up and down simultaneously clapping his hands and echoes jubilantly, *"I lose! I lose!"*

Giggling, they start the circle again and again — same result, same happy reply, *"I lose! I lose!"* How could I help laughing out loud? The tension that had been mounting all day began its descent.

As I sit here, writing and enjoying the memory of the evening, I don't remember whether I ended up burning the garlic bread. I don't remember if the pasta was mush. I don't remember if I achieved the high standard of domesticity desired. I do know that my world of hurried busyness was beautifully interrupted by a juvenile profundity.

How many times in any given day to I compare myself to others? How often do I beat myself up because I just don't seem to be "doing life" as well as my neighbor? Someone always has a cleaner house, a bigger savings account, a better marriage. Someone is always ahead of me in the race and I *feel* like a loser.

For Timmy, it wasn't about the winning or losing — it was about *running*. It was the excitement of the chase, laughing at himself when he fell and picking himself up again. It was trying over and over again — ignoring the labels. It was about doing the best *he* could, running as fast as *his* own little legs can carry him, all the while not resenting the person ahead. And all that from a two-year-old.

Lord, help me to have the heart of a child — to not take myself so seriously. Oh, that I would finish the race, not comparing myself to others, and with utter abandoned proclaim with pride, *I lose! I lose!*

He called a little child and had him stand among them.
And He said, "I tell you the truth,
Unless you change and become like little children,
You will never enter the kingdom of heaven.
Therefore, whoever humbles himself like this child
Is the greatest in the kingdom of heaven.

Matthew 18: 2-4

December 28, 1999

Well, Christmas is over and New Year's is just a few days away. Right now I am terrible. I have been able to function and deal with life by just staying focused on the holidays and Michael being home. Now, it is all over and reality has hit me like a load of bricks! I just put the kids to bed and as usual, did so in a frustrated, non-loving way. I am absolutely amazed! I have worked hard all day (with the exception of a rest I took when the kids were down for naps). This house is a disaster! I really can't imagine other people living this way. I cleaned the upstairs bathroom. I started a lot of projects today and finished none. I feel like I have been in the dark forever. If something doesn't change soon, I know I'm not going to make it. Something dreadful is going to happen. Either I'm going to desert my family in an irrational state or snap and be institutionalized ... or die. I just cannot live like this anymore. I think I must be dying. I tried to explain to Michael how I feel by using the analogy of a mother who is told she has to abort her baby or she is going to die. She can't in good conscience kill her baby and yet she is doomed to certain death. I love my children desperately. I am just physically not able to be a good mother, wife and homemaker. I am doomed to be a disaster. I AM a disaster. And I would rather not live, than live as a disaster. I am so tired. I feel as if I can't even hold my head up. God, I ask that You would bring me out of this deep, deep pit. You are all powerful and You love me. If You do not work a miracle ... I see no way out. Heal my mind. Heal my body. I ask that Jesus' blood would cover me. I'm not even sure what that means. But I know that I can't get to You unless I go through Jesus. Help me dear Lord.

Heidi

The Christmas Miracle

It was Christmas Eve and we were all nestled in row at our annual candlelight service at New Song Christian Fellowship. I was feeling relaxed — happy that we were all together. Not just my four children and husband, but my in-laws as well. This was an unusual church service. It wasn't because of the lovely Christmas lights strung from ceiling to floor. It wasn't the casual unscripted message that was delivered by my pastor. It wasn't even the fact that my father-in-law, a staunch agnostic, decided to take communion with us. It was unusual because of the state of my family!

I proudly inspected them. They were each neatly bathed, hair-combed, teeth brushed and shoes polished! If that weren't enough — my three boys wore their freshly pressed, matching red and white, candy striped shirts, and Meghan, Michael and I were *color coordinated*! I was *prepared!* The moment one of my little flock started to get restless, I could reach into my bag of tricks where there was an assortment of activities, juice and treats; all meant to sooth the savage beasts just waiting to possess my children at any moment and disrupt the service.

Sitting just in front of me was a lovely family of five: a husband, wife, two young daughters and a son, which if I ventured a guess, was around two-years-old. As the evening progressed from Christmas carols to sermon, my children, strangely enough, were angelic. But I observed the family in front of me who began the evening with *Joy to the World* in their hearts, descend into the pit of lost expectations.

Surely you know what I mean. You envision the candlelight … the harmony … the inspiration as the pastor helps you to focus on the true meaning of Christmas … aglow with good will toward men. Then the reality hits — fifteen minutes into the sermon you're excusing yourself for the third time to discipline your four-year-old for smacking his brother up-side the head. His screams are amplified to the tenth degree as you hastily make your way through throngs of people to the exit.

A similar scenario was being played out in front of me — and blessing of blessings — I was able to be of some service. I reached into my goodie-bag and produced a trinket that seemed to placate the little toddler, much to the relief of his mother.

The evening was gratefully coming to a close and approaching the moment we had all been anticipating. Each person would get to hold a little white candle — one by one, row by row, they are lit — resulting in the whole room being illuminated by a chorus of tiny flames. What ambiance! What serenity! *Silent night, holy night, all is calm, all is bright;* until some little hand gets burned by the melting wax and hollers.

This year it wasn't a little hand that belonged to me. It was the precious little Dutch-blonde in front of me, whom I had already appeased once. His shrieks filled the rafters. This is when you find out how effective your antiperspirant is. Mom and Dad passed him back and forth trying to comfort him to no avail. They were trapped and any attempts to escape the center of their row might pose a worse fire hazard.

Faster than a speeding bullet … da, da, tah, dah … Super-mom to the rescue! I swooped in with the universal, pediatric-approved anesthetic …. candy! One of those chewy peppermint taffies with the little green Christmas tree in the center. Within seconds the sobs subsided, tears were wiped away and we were all able to get through till dismissal, with our nerves in tact.

Afterwards the grateful parents were apologetic and gushed with praise. I immediately assured them that they had just witnessed a Christmas miracle. I was *actually* able to minister to someone else in a small way. It seems that over the past 11 years I have always been the one in the receiving chair, where some kind-hearted, together-for-the-moment, person comes to my aid. It truly is a joy to have an overflow — an abundance to share.

I have been forced into learning the art of being a gracious recipient and it has been good for my character. But let me say, it is no fun being in perpetual poverty! I'm not necessarily talking about money, although it certainly can be included. It seems that in recent years I have been bankrupt — bankrupt of time — bankrupt of energy — bankrupt of patience. Lord, thank You for this Christmas Eve. It was You who enabled me to prioritize and organize. It was You that gave me more than enough. I pray that in this new year I may have ample opportunities to be a blessing!

> **For we are God's workmanship, created in**
> **Christ Jesus to do good works, which**
> **God prepared in advance for us to do.**
>
> **Ephesians 2:10**

October 10, 2001

I am so unhappy — so sick inside — so tired of feeling this way. I feel like all my dreams are killing me, my dreams of love, romance, career. I am an all or nothing person. If I decide I need to cut back on sweets then I have to throw anything with sugar out of the house. As long as I have these dreams of being a singer/ songwriter, I will be continually disappointed and discontented. There is a part of me that wants to cast it all into the sea and never talk about it again. But how do you completely distance yourself from those dreams if the reality is continually flaunted in your face? Michael is a continual reminder of my lost expectations. Right now I want to go burn all my songs — to have a ceremony where I can symbolically die to all of those dreams. The drive for greatness is so rooted in me. I fear my life will be meaningless without my dreams. I think of different people in my life, examples of squandered time. Years – money – energy — on extreme goals. Do I want to be like that? Am I already like that? I'm afraid the answer is yes. Godliness with contentment is great gain. I want to throw myself full throttle into going to school in January — no more of this piddling around. A degree is an achievable goal! It is a dream where 2 + 2 = 4! If I study and make good grades … I will graduate. And when I get a degree I will be able to have a career. Provided God keeps me alive, breathing in and out, being a counselor is up to me. With all the problems in marriages and families, the need for Christian counselors is going to be great! Here is a future! Lord Jesus, help me in this endeavor.

Heidi

School Days

Today, I did one of the bravest things of my life! At age thirty-two, mother of four, I went back to school — college to be exact.

After searching for a parking place like hidden treasure, I walked for what might possibly have been a *literal* mile, just to stand in the middle of I knew not where. Buildings and sidewalks spread in every direction. I pondered all of the obstacles I had already hurdled just to get to this place and time: childcare, money, support from my husband, also coming to terms with the fact that Michael and I were never going to be Sonny & Cher or the Osmond family.

The years of frantically bailing water out of a sinking ship of dreams. Now, I was swimming to shore on an uncharted island, a paradise with promise. But there I was with a new and seemingly insurmountable obstacle — reading my campus map! Utterly and completely lost, I stared and strained at the paper before me, turning it this way and that. Unaware and intensely focused, I was startled by a kind young man, and an experienced student, who had tuned in to my silent distress signals. He led me through a maze to the entrance of the student center and bookstore. I thanked him, my merciful guiding angel.

Inside the bookstore awaited a sea of bodies, lines and more lines, and much to my dismay, further opportunities for independent thinking. I longed for the familiarity of Target, with my typed, black and white supplies list: Elmer's glue, blunt-tipped scissors, colored construction paper. I remembered the feeling of my daughter's hand in mine as we meandered down the aisles discussing the pro's and con's of a *Lisa Frank* lunch box as opposed to *Barbie*.

"Snap out of it!" I wrestled myself back to reality. "I think I can … I think I can."

Rows of books loomed before me, but with perseverance I found my *one* textbook for my *one* class. Next, I waited in a line more in keeping with an amusement park than a bookstore. With my textbook (that cost a small fortune) in hand I made my way back through the glass doors and directed my feet towards class.

How could I be an adult, approaching middle age, and still feel like a five-year old with pig-tails on the first day of kindergarten? Excited — terrified! Driven to push forward — the impulse to run away! Feeling vulnerable I yearned for the safety of home. Picking up my cell phone, I rang Michael.

He listened amused as I whimpered and whined. We were both surprised by my childish uncertainty. After all, isn't this what I had been longing for? Little could he understand, or I foresee, how great I would feel the divide, the canyon that had been forged over the last fourteen years! Going back to any school would have been daunting, but MTSU with over 20,000 students?

My private Christian high school boasted that ours, the class of 1987, was the largest graduating class in its history. We had around sixty-five graduates and an overall enrollment of approximately 200. Middle Tennessee State University was a population increase of 100%! If that weren't enough to intimidate, I must also mention over the past years I have accrued a variety of labels including: anxiety disorder, panic disorder, and depression just to name a few. Resulting from these lovely epithets, is an extreme distaste for crowds or anything that would trigger a phobic behavior. It is not uncommon for me to thoroughly arrange my schedule in such a way as to completely avoid large groups of people.

Having given you just the amount of information that seems necessary — here is the good news — the miracle! I did it! I didn't run! By God's grace, I pressed through! Through the procrastination, through the accusatory voices that regularly bombarded my head shouting condemnation like, "You'll never stick with it. You're just setting yourself up for failure. You'll fail like you fail everything else. You're just going to find out how stupid you really are!"

I navigated through the mental bombing and stood my ground unto experiencing my first class ... General Psychology, the first victory over many battles ahead. It is a long, narrow and rocky path toward the final goal — a Master's degree. I may not get there until I'm officially old and gray. But *over-the-hill* will have a much sweeter meaning for me because over that hill is a valley where I will be qualified and licensed to work in the area of counseling and church ministry. It is just one step forward. By God, I did it!

Have I not commanded you?
Be strong and courageous.
Do not be terrified; do not be discouraged,
For the Lord your God will be with you wherever you go.

Joshua 1:9

June 7, 2001

My soul is in anguish. I am rejected. I have been betrayed by those I love and trust the most. In turn I have once again failed You, and them, by taking that pain out on those closest to me. Oh God, I have faith that You hear me and are intimately acquainted with suffering. Help me to have the faith that You love me and do not condemn. But that somehow, where physical arms are not there to hold me together, mystically there are arms without flesh that can wrap around what is not body and hold my spirit fast. Oh how I wish You could come in the flesh and physically hold me right now—to rock me and say that I am beautiful, lovely, precious, unique — that all of my ugliness will not scare You away. I can assent mentally that these things are true of You. But oh how I long for a man of flesh to touch me — for an audible voice to speak words of kindness — to be caressed, nurtured, cherished. I am so afraid of losing Michael's affections, and in fact I believe I have. But I have not yet lost his word and covenant of faithfulness. Help me Lord. Hold the hurt and rejected part of me still so that I will not further push Michael away. Help me to care for our children and teach them of You in the middle of this crisis. God I ask for a miracle! I ask for more than Michael's will, I ask for his heart. I feel as if I cannot bear his disdain. I panic and though I feel this should stir compassion and mercy, it only provokes repulsion from him. Help me to see the beauty in me. Help Michael to see the beauty in me. Direct my path, put the words in my heart that need to be said. Have compassion on me my Lord and my God.

Heidi

Sacred Love

Today I want to express my thoughts on the person most dear to me in all the world … my husband Michael. This is a topic that I approach with caution. How do I write about the intimate, sacred love that I feel for the man I am one with? I am afraid that I will fail miserably but I cannot suppress the desire to try.

I *love* my husband! The exclamation point is representative of intensity not volume. In fact, if I were to speak it right now it would be in a hushed tone — a whisper. I am going to imagine that I am in an empty, ancient, grand cathedral where even the smallest tap of a shoe bounces off every wall. In awe I speak …

Lord, thank you for a man who remains true to his vow. He has stayed with me through "better" and "worse," even though recently the worse seems to swallow up any memory of the better. Thank you for the way he still makes me feel like his girlfriend — not a wife of thirteen years — when he unashamedly shows public displays of affection. I love the way he wraps his arm around me at church and pulls me close, then bends his head down to give me a light feather-kiss on my cheek, as if he is claiming his territory. I like that. Thank you for giving me a man that fiercely protects me against anyone who might bring me harm even if it is family or friends. In fact, he might as well hang a sign around my neck that says, "You mess with her, you mess with me." You must have known how much the little girl in me needed that kind of safety.

Even now blurred with tears, I thank you for his kind and thoughtful ways that I so easily take for granted. Like taking the kids out to McDonalds to relieve my nerves. When we go to the Sub Stop, or a similar restaurant, I don't even think about it, I go sit down while he waits in line, orders our food, then brings it to me with all the appropriate utensils. He is washing my feet.

Thank you for the sacrifice he has made in time and money to send me back to school. While I'm on the subject, thank you so much, that he supports sending our children to a Christian school knowing how important that is to me. Thank you for a man who has remained faithful when I was taught that all men would eventually cheat on their wives.

Thank you for a man who is always striving to better himself … intellectually, spiritually, emotionally and physically. Thank you that he is interested in making our marriage a priority and chooses to spend time with me on a weekly date. For this and so much more I am grateful! Help us in our hour of need. Bring us through stronger and with a love deeper than we have ever known. Amen.

**Wives, submit to your husbands as to the Lord.
Husbands, love your wives, just as
Christ loved the church and gave himself up for her.
He who loves his wife loves himself.**

Ephesians 4: 22,25 & 28

September 26, 1998

Lord, I just feel the need to write down all of my fears and give them to you tonight.

1) *Fear of my husband cheating on me.*
2) *Fear of my husband leaving me.*
3) *Fear of rejection not being liked or loved by my husband.*
4) *Fear of becoming unattractive.*
5) *Fear of not getting it "right" with you. That somehow I might be wrong in my understanding and be lost to hell.*
6) *Fear of your disapproval.*
7) *Fear of my children rejecting/not respecting me.*
8) *Fear that I'm not doing enough for my children — praying enough — teaching enough — paying enough attention to them.*
9) *Fear of my disease.*
10) *Fear of sudden calamity.*
11) *Fear of never getting through this time.*
12) *Fear of the end-times (end of the world).*
13) *Fear of never being "good" at anything.*
14) *Fear of dying.*
15) *Fear of people thinking I "don't" have it all together.*
16) *Fear of people not needing me.*

Heidi

Faith and Angels

When Adam and Eve ate the fruit of the tree that brought both the knowledge of good and evil, their black and white world fell off the edge into oblivion. Never again would there be a day in Adam's life when fear did not lurk somewhere in the shadows of his mind. He had been officially introduced to evil and now could not escape the acquaintance.

Gone were the days of frolicking through each day unencumbered. Now, when his sons went out to play he would have to instruct them to be sure to be home by dark, knowing the wild beasts that hunt at night. I can see him looking into Cain's eyes, "Son, poke a stick at that pile of leaves before you and Abel go jumping in!" He knew that though it may be tempting to pounce and stomp through the brush and feel the crackle between their toes, a deadly viper may lie in wait to sink its fangs into their tiny callous heals. It has been innumerable generations since that fateful day and we have all been tainted by the fall.

Fear has been a dominating sin in my life. Sometimes I feel its control more than others. There have been times when I've crowed – DELIVERANCE — only to discover a new realm where he reigns. Sometimes he shows up when my husband is traveling and I awake in the middle of the night tormented by the thought of some "cracked-up maniac" breaking through the door with an automatic weapon.

There are other thoughts that quite frankly, I'm embarrassed to even admit. But let's just say I have to be very careful about movies that I watch or they will come back to haunt me (i.e., *Signs*). These negative mental images can completely freak me out and I will get up several times, compulsively checking my doors over and over to see if they are locked. Other fears have been airplanes, my husband leaving me, crocodiles, swimming in the ocean, cruise ships … the list could go on. But I am reminded of me, as an18 year old girl, who in this instance stepped on the neck of the serpent.

It was around twelve-midnight and I was on my way back to an unsavory part of New Jersey where my singing group was stationed. Feeling awkward and exposed, (never having been anywhere on a city bus alone or out so late) I tried to soothe myself with the memories of the day.

My cousin, Totsie, had charmed me with New York City life, sampling all its delights: Central Park, hotdogs from a real New York street vendor, bagels, cheesecake, Macy's and even a ride on the subway. As a Texas native these novelties made the "Big Apple" virtually a new country.

The bus came to a screeching stop and my drop off point was just short of my destination. I still had to walk approximately a mile to the hotel, in complete darkness with a few street lamps a considerable ways off.

Laden with packages, I knew I had "victimize me" stamped right across my forehead! Starting my journey, I was uncomfortably aware that my heart was attempting to escape from my chest. Thump! Thump! Thump! I put one wobbly foot in front of the other. Suddenly I was inspired to sing a familiar song from my childhood:

All night—all Day
Angel's watching over me my Lord
All night—all day
Angel's watching over me

Over and over I repeated the chorus, not remembering anything else. Here's the cool thing — I BELIEVED IT! My heart started beating with less aggression and my feet moved with more purpose. I sang loud and with confidence — convinced that if any murdering, rapist, thug should encounter me — he would see one, if not several big, burly, white men, who of course would be my personally assigned bouncer-angels! It was sort of a David and Goliath faith overcoming any doubt.

Is it possible that when we are children we are allotted a certain quotient of "Eden?" And the older we get, the more we pile on the knowledge of both good and evil and the harder it is to access that kind of trust? In my quest to become a great thinker and philosopher — to approach life with logic and reason — my faith in what is unseen, untouchable, unfathomable is choked into near extinction. Lord, let me have the wisdom of Solomon and still retain the impenetrable faith of David.

When I am afraid,
I will trust in You.
In God, whose word I praise,
In God I trust; I will not be afraid.
What can mortal man do to me?

Psalm 56:3&4

September 30, 2001

My life is a complete mess. I am in a continual war and just trying to survive day to day without seriously scarring my children. I love them. I don't think I like children in general though. I look forward to the day when we can be friends, but I'm afraid they will not want to be my friend once they are older because they will resent all of my struggles in their childhoods. I have often thought life is so screwy. We go to school when we are young and don't really care about learning. We have no sense of who we are in college and this is when we usually decide our careers and life partners. I look back on my life and I see one major decision after another that I treated with as much gravity as what to wear to a party. I married — and had baby after baby without much thought. I allowed my present feelings to dictate my life's course. Now, here I am with no real answers. I want to do what I have always done — throw caution to the wind and go for the immediate gratification. You would think that I would have learned by now. Right now every muscle in my body wants to run — run away — away from all these problems, away from all these chains. Run and find something or someone to heal this horrible pain in my gut. Many times I have surveyed my life and have come to the same conclusion. I am not a better person today than when I was seventeen. In fact, I like that person much better. That is just backward. I have exhausted every doorway. I know I am on a sure path to depression if You do not intervene, Lord. I hardly know how to pray. I know that You see my marriage and that it is Your desire that Michael and I stay together. Help me to love him for who he is and not what I would have him to be. Help me to see the treasure of his love. Help me to enjoy my children more. Help me to realize what I have got before it is gone. I am in desperate need of major heart surgery because every aspect of my life is drudgery and a burden. I don't want my children growing up feeling like they are burdens. I want them to feel wanted and that my life is better, richer and more beautiful because they are in it. Dear Lord, help Michael to forgive my past mistakes. Help me to experience Your love in a greater way so I won't feel so alone. I half believe it cannot be done — help my unbelief. Help me to be morally strong and courageous — to not fall into the continual temptations that are before me. Help me Jesus—for You are strong and I am weak.

Heidi

Hilarious Hurricanes

How many of you think that your life is secretly the inspiration for a family sitcom? That somehow there are hidden cameras everywhere, linked to a satellite in space where your footage is then fed into the creative offices of NBC, ABC and FOX networks. Sitcoms take ordinary life situations and over exaggerate them so that we can all laugh at ridiculous human nature, only in my case it is *not* an exaggeration but rather a documentary. Let me explain…

It was a blustery day, hurricane Irene was passing through Nashville and they were predicting wind gusts with the power to knock down trees and sheets of rain being slung to the earth. I, being in body and spirit, inflexible, decided that the inconvenient weather was not going to deter my outing to Target. It was a needed escape from the four brick walls of my prison house. Target was one of my favorite destinations, not necessarily with my two-year old, but Michael was out of town and beggars can't always be choosers.

We managed to get there safely. I stepped out of my car door with an umbrella in hand, slapped on my backpack, then removed Timmy from his car seat and rested him squarely on my hip as we proceeded to the automatic doors. We were in good humor, both of us happy for the change in scenery. With one arm fastened around him and another placed on the umbrella I asked Timmy to help and he was delighted to comply. Giggling quietly, the wind pulled us upward just like Mary Poppins, only to turn and sweep beneath our shelter to spray our faces with a light, cool *Evian*-like mist. The rain danced merrily at our feet. Our steps were quick, keeping time with the cadence of the rain.

Soon we were inside and in the shopping groove, leisurely going down each aisle. Timmy sat in the basket appeased with a slurpee and a small bag of popcorn. One after the other, I added those necessary items (the one's I couldn't possibly live without) into the basket. It wasn't long before it was piled high with pillows and pantyhose. All too soon, Timmy had consumed his treats and was growing impatient with his restraints.

I was in need of a little more space, so making a colossal mistake, I said in the sweetest little voice, "Timmy … Mommy will put you down if you will stay with me, right next to the basket … okay?"

The first warning flag that my pleasant morning was about to end was raised in his emphatic response, "NO!"

I replied firmly, "Timmy — say '*Yes* Mommy'," and down he came.

The rest of my time was spent fussing, nagging and bribing a two-year old to behave in a way that is improbable, if not impossible, for a healthy, toddler boy on the loose. After all, what are those child restraints on the baskets for? Several times he decided to play hide-and-seek on our way through the check out line.

Now I was becoming a spectacle and object of judgment. Prying eyes were fastened on me as I yelled for Timmy to show himself immediately! I wanted to get home now as expediently as possible. No longer did my abode with its predictable environment seem stifling, but more like a welcome sanctuary. Little giggles and kind tones had been vanquished. Now all that remained was a stressed, embarrassed mother squeezing the hand of a screaming child as we made our way towards the exit and the now raging weather.

Before me lay a problem. How was I going to get my over-loaded basket, my child and myself to the car, while holding an umbrella to protect us from the elements, without being swept away? I saw no other option. I simply must carry my son, so I proceeded to shove things into every functional crevice of my body and with a push of a button my umbrella inflated and I waited for just the right moment.

"We can do this!" I stated to a doubting Timmy.

"Okay … Okay … Okay…"

Tension mounted. "GO!"

No sooner had I stepped out than a gust of wind knocked me off balance causing me to lose control of the heavily weighed down basket. Off it went down the slope into the parking lot, items falling into what was now a river underfoot. Chasing after the fugitive buggy, jostling Timmy up and down, the rain no longer danced, but drove forcefully into my eyes limiting my already obstructed vision.

Just at a critical moment — when you think your situation could not be any more challenging — that devious wind literally reached in and turned my umbrella inside out! I, having no available appendages to correct this perversion, began to seriously entertain the temptation to be a potty-mouth.

There we were, being whipped about, drenched in a downpour, when out of the corner of my eye I spied two strapping young employees of Target. To my dismay they just sat there, observing my plight with little sympathy. I bent to pick up the soaked articles only to drop another. Timmy was now wailing. Imploringly I looked at them again, bodily speaking volumes, yet they were unmoved!

After what seemed like an eternity, I finally gathered my belongings and tossed babe and baggage into the truck and resumed my position behind the wheel … dripping, disheartened and down right disturbed! How could they have just stood there? How could they have restrained themselves from helping?

The water began to evaporate off the top of my head like a black-paved road after a summer storm. I was steaming with righteous indignation! Then as if a rewind button was pushed, the scene, play-by-play, rolled across my imagination just as if I was sitting on the couch on a Monday night, cuddled up next to my husband. Moments like Lucy Ricardo shoving chocolates into her mouth as fast as she can while the conveyer belt produces more candies to wrap than are "wrappable." Or Gilligan hanging on to a palm tree for dear life as the wind stretches him out like superman. I started to giggle. Giggling turned into chuckling and chuckling into peels of laughter.

Timmy's tears turned to joy not even knowing why. All the way home I thought about how messy life is — unpredictable and chaotic! Thank You, Lord, for the ability to laugh at ourselves. Thank You for teaching us lessons all the time. For example, the next time a hurricane breezes through town, think twice before leaving the comforts of home. But Lord, if it is not too sinful, may I request that those Target-boys get fired?

There is a time for everything,
And a season for every activity under heaven:
A time to be born and a time to die,
A time to plant and a time to uproot,
A time to kill and a time to heal,
A time to tear down and a time to build,
A time to weep and a time to laugh,
A time to mourn and a time to dance.

Ecclesiastes 3:1-4

May 2, 2005

Today I am reading Mark 7 and I feel the leading of the Holy Spirit to write some things down. This week on Thursday is National Day of Prayer and I was explaining to the children on the way to school that it is not enough to recognize our sin and be sorry. Repentance involves a turning away from sin, then God will heal our land. I cannot control others and their choices but I feel pressed in my spirit to ask God to reveal my sin. Where have I set up idols in my heart and home? As I have been reading in the Old Testament — over and over again — the Israelites didn't get it. Even when they turned back to the Lord, they still left "Asherah poles" and the "high places" where they worshiped. Even Solomon succumbed because of his foreign wives. The wisest man who ever lived! I long to break free from those sins that hold me back and yet there is a hidden part of me that fears what God will require of me. As I was in Mark 7:15, Jesus says "Nothing outside a man can make him 'unclean'." Immediately I was convicted of my sin. Out of the overflow of the heart the mouth speaks, and so much of the time I speak critical words about so many people. My tongue is so out of control that it is like an airborne virus. I used to reason that it doesn't matter if it is in your heart — you might as well speak it, because God sees the heart and you have already sinned. But now I know that is Satan's lie. If I contain and only pour my negativity out to God then at least it only affects me and God can deal with me. When those words are released and go into others' ears, I am contaminating the air and spreading the sin to others whose immunity is down. May God show mercy and kindness to me, His servant, and cleanse me from all unrighteousness as He has promised.

Heidi

Washing Cycles

What a glorious day in the Lord! Once again He has spoken to me in a most unexpected way and through such ordinary life-stuff.

Today, as most days, I had a lot on my plate. One of my major responsibilities was to tackle the pile of laundry that was challenging Mount Everest in elevation. But before I could scale the Alp's I had a more pressing engagement. Michael and I have been reading <u>Purpose Driven Life</u> by Rick Warren. He recommends that you commit to it for forty days and that is what we are attempting. What a delicious season I am in … sitting with my lover, sipping sweet "creamery" coffee, as we seek the Lord together and talk about what we have learned. Truly, does it get any better? Our reading today was rich with meaning. No matter how long we have been disciples of Christ, it never hurts to have a refresher course and that's what Mr. Warren's book is — *Christianity 101.*

After our morning date, I rolled up my sleeves and got to work. Around lunchtime, the Spirit kept drawing my heart back to the Word. Though time was ticking and my mountain was unmoved, I was obedient. I devoured my readings in II Kings and Mark — bowing my head as I asked the Lord to help me digest all I had taken in. I was so full it felt like I had just "scarffed" down a Thanksgiving banquet. Pushing my chair away from the table, I knew I couldn't hold one more bite. As I took another moment for prayer, I very clearly heard the Lord admonish me to rest — literally to lay down on the bed and close my eyes.

I heard about a conversation one time that went something like this:

"You say God *told* you to do this and God *told* you to do that. Do you hear the Lord audibly?"

The man replied, "Oh no ... *much* louder than that!"

Hearing the Lord is a mystery and I am far from mastering discernment, but I try to listen and obey as best as I can.

"Lord," I said. "I have already indulged so much today. This can't be right! This is bordering on laziness!"

But the impression remained. I quickly went to the laundry room and threw in a load of particularly soiled whites. I have no comprehension how little boys manage to get as filthy as they do. This was no ordinary load of laundry; the only course of action was the hot soak cycle and bleach. I pushed the button and in obedience proceeded to take a nap.

For a while I just lay there, breathing deeply, making an effort to control my thoughts. Concentrating on phrases like: God is just, God is faithful, God is merciful. I inhaled and exhaled.

"How long am I supposed to do this?" I wondered.

And the Holy Spirit whispered ... *I'll let you know* ... and I drifted off.

I was roused sometime later hardly even realizing what had taken place, to the sound of the soak cycle transitioning to spin. Once again He spoke in such tenderness. *Heidi, just like those clothes, you needed time to soak. There are stains in you that go so deep ... fear, unforgiveness, contempt ... they are ground in and need the right environment to come clean. It is rest that you need; rest from your works, rest from your anxieties. Let Me do the work for you.*

You cannot imagine how refreshed I was — how clean. You also cannot believe how God multiplied my efforts, just like the bread and the fish (John 6). I was able to accomplish all that was necessary for the day. Life happens and not every day can go as beautifully as this one did, but I think I've been given a glimpse of what Jesus meant when He talked about *abundant life*. Mmmm ... more *please!*

**I have come that they may have *life*, and have it to the *full*.
John 10:10**

January 16, 2007

I have had such a rich morning in the Lord. My time in the Word was so rewarding — I literally hugged and kissed my Bible. Every time I pick it up, there is the possibility of an encounter with my God and my Jesus. I am so amazed after tasting the sweetness of the cup of the Lord, how easy it still is to crave refreshment from the world, even when I know it will not satisfy. I must confess that a good portion of my thoughts are given to the temporal, even sinful things. I continually pine after fame and all the benefits that result from it. I would like to be "somebody" and enjoy all the special privileges that come from a title. Just as Christ warned of the yeast of the Pharisees, who like to be greeted in the marketplace and have the seats of honor, if I am honest, I crave to eat of that bread. I know I want my life to bring Jesus glory, but it is mixed with a generous dose of a desire for personal glory too. But God has promised through John 1:9 (what wonderful words), "If we confess our sins He is faithful and just and will forgive and purify us from all unrighteousness." I trust that He is transforming my heart to be more like His. Another big glitch in my Christian walk is my compassion for the lost. Most times I would be content to live a version of a solitary monk's life — to spend my hours and days alone with God — absorbing His Word, immersing myself in study and writing. I would only come out for breaks to walk and commune with nature. I don't necessarily want to deal with people. As much as I would like to convince myself that this is okay, I know in my spirit it is not. So here we are, back to the balance of life. We are all uniquely created with a unique role to fulfill. I am intent on discovering what that is today, and as far into the future as the Lord will reveal. The great cry of my heart is to hear my Lord say to me, "Well done, good and faithful servant."

Heidi

The Benevolent Biker

The Lord is so good! He is everywhere, incessantly communicating to us. Unfortunately, much of the time I go through life with my eyes shut to His signs and my ears closed to His instruction. It's not out of purposeful rebellion, it is simply that I'm overbooked. I'm in a hurry. I'm distracted. I tune Him out just like I do my children.

It is not an exaggeration when I confess that there are many instances where Timmy or Joseph will stand right under my feet saying, "Mom…Mom…Mom." It may take ten or more times for me to even realize they are there (much to my husband's chagrin). How many times does the Lord have to call my name before I am aroused from my stupor and say, "Speak Lord, for your servant is listening" (I Samuel 3)? I thank God for His patience when He continues to call, way past ten to eleven, twelve and so on … until I look up.

We are blessed to have a friend who has a home in the mountains and a condo at the beach. And because of his generosity, this past October, Michael and I took our children out of school for a week and went on holiday. I just love the way that sounds—so British. It was our first time in the Daytona Beach area as a family and the kids were looking forward to the sand and surf.

The sand had been replaced with millions of tiny broken pieces of shells. This was a little rough on the feet, but to our delight, scattered among the gravel were little treasures waiting to be discovered. We scoured up and down the coast filling our buckets so full that we were able to make shell necklaces on our return home for all the little one's classmates. We boogey boarded, we ate at *Bubba Gump's*, we miniature golfed, we *vacationed!* There was one small hindrance to completely abandoning ourselves to hedonism ... the noise!!!

Because of the many storms that had recently hit the Florida coast, the lounging area outside our condominium was literally covered in beach. The day we came, the waves were rolling into and over the pool lapping straight up to the patio doors underneath our second floor balcony. After several days of excavation, the caretaker began to reveal a lost city under the mounds of sand and shells. There were cobblestone paths, lavish landscaping, even a putting green (which consequently was completely restored the morning we left). We were told that there were even six stairs, going down to the actual beach, which still remained entombed.

But this lonely, elderly groundskeeper would never be able to finish the job on his own; he had to call in the big guns. In came the machinery: the "whooshers" and diggers, the spinners, blowers and "broomers" (these are all very complicated and technical terms). And though we appreciated the fact that they needed to do their jobs, at times, the desired atmosphere was spoiled.

There were few people vacationing besides us, being that it was the middle of the workweek and in October. Our only companions were an eccentric group of Hell's Angels attending an annual gathering called "Biketoberfest." Never having run in the circle of "biker people," stereotypes of wild, rebellious heathens dominated my thoughts. It was probably best for my family and me to keep our distance. If approached by one of these wild beasts, be very still and maybe they would just sniff and go away.

Each day I would see them congregate at the disheveled pool area to relax, soak in the rays, chit-chat and throw back a few cold ones. As I sat on my balcony attempting to have my quiet time, *attempting* being the operative word, I wondered how I might be a witness to them … the bikers. Maybe they had noticed me on my terrace reading my Bible. Maybe I should be like Daniel and get on my knees and pray right there so they could see my good works and praise God in heaven? If only those IRRITATING workers would CEASE their interminable RACKET!!!

It was then that I noticed the scantily clad, bronzed biker-chick leave her lounge chair and disappear through her sliding glass doors. She shortly returned carrying some refreshment in her hands. She walked towards her comrades, but continued on, past her chair onto the newly swept path, directly towards the sweaty proletarian that was working the obnoxious "whoosher." He paused then turned off the monstrosity. Words were exchanged. He smiled and took the cup from her hand.

SMACK! How could a cup of cold water feel like a sound spanking? There I was basking in my misplaced piety, coddling myself in a coveted ritual. Seeking to know His Word when the Word became flesh right before my very eyes! A sobering reminder that all the scripture reading in the world does me no good if it is not converted into action. God is a faithful, involved Father who disciplines the children He loves. Thank You Father, for Your tender correction.

If anyone has material possessions
and sees his brother in need
But has no pity on him, how can
the love of God be in him?
Dear children, let us not love with words or tongue
But with actions and in truth.

1 John 3:17&18

Contentment (2001)

Today is the day,
It is time.
Time for Dream to say good-bye;
To let you go
Let you fly.
Fly away to someone new
Who'll maybe more your justice do;
And lighting there
Realize what you were meant to be.

When you go
There'll be no rest,
To feel the hole
Within my breast;
Relief mixed in with bitterness
For life to you I clung.
Upon my neck
A rope was hung,
And now for life
Must be undone
For death is at my door.

I'm searching for a kinder friend
If Peace should come
I'd let him in,
And all I have to him I'd give
Who bore the name
Contentment.

Heidi

Godliness with Contentment

Paul said to Timothy, "Godliness with contentment is great gain" (1 Timothy 6:6). There was a time in the early years of our marriage when we would have fallen into the lowest income bracket. Meghan, my firstborn, was a baby and I was determined to stay at home with her, even though up until that time I had been the main provider. Neither Michael nor I were qualified to do much when we moved to Nashville for Michael to pursue music. So as most aspiring musicians in Music City, he joined the chain gang — as in restaurant chain.

As a waiter he provided just enough to cover our basic needs. The roof over our head was, well let's just say *adequate* — a run down, two-bedroom apartment in a questionable part of town. As you looked out our sliding glass doors onto our slab patio, the view was of a concrete-block retaining wall. It appeared as if we were underground. The main entrance to our home was not directly accessible. Like a dormitory, you would enter through a side door into a gray-green dimly lit hall, with popcorn water-stained ceilings and blinking florescent lights. The brass numbers on our door were tarnished and by the multiple coats of paint sloppily applied you could probably determine the age of the building, just like the rings in the stump of a tree.

Inside our little dwelling it was aged but neat. There was some new furniture, a couch and table that we had purchased pre-baby, that stood out by its crispness, along with a few hand-me-downs and cheap plywood assembly-required accent pieces from Walmart. Sometimes I look back and think ... *tacky* ... but I have to say, I had a healthy sense of pride in our tiny abode.

110

Thirteen years later, we have added three more children and well over two thousand more square feet. There is also another digit added to our income tax returns. Michael is no longer a starving artist although he is still a waiter of sorts, serving people the bread of life, rather than yeast rolls. I am still a stay at home mom, but with many more luxuries. I now make Kraft macaroni and cheese out of choice (my three boys love it) rather than for economy sake.

Through the passage of time, things have greatly changed in terms of money and stuff, but I understand now — having been a part of different levels of social classification — what Paul was saying. As I reflect on my life, the experience of happiness and pleasure was never diminished when I was poor. There was nothing added or subtracted to our marriage bed whether we were on a queen-size mattress with Kmart's bed-in-a-bag, or our beautiful four-poster king with duvet and feathers. Seeing my daughter take her first steps could not have been heightened if she had been walking on polished mahogany floors, rather than the scratchy building-grade carpet. Joy was joy in its full measure.

And on the flip side, pain was pain, sorrow was sorrow and anger is just as destructive under the roof of a mansion as well as a hovel. I have learned that in my *flesh*, enough is never enough. It is a lie when I say, "Oh, if I could only have more space ... then I would keep it clean." Or, "Once I get a new sofa, a proper room for entertaining, a housekeeper ... *then* I'll open up my home for God's purposes." We are who we are. Life is essentially made up of the same ingredients, at least in America. In the verse below Paul uses the well-chosen word *secret.* Secret ... something not everyone knows, it is hidden, only revealed to a chosen few.

Believe it or not, now I struggle with guilt. It is like a no-win situation. Allowing myself to enjoy God's material blessings is hard for me. I walk around tormented, feeling that there must be something horribly sinful in the abundance that surrounds me. Thankfully, this is also addressed by Paul. Satan wants to trap us any way he can. If he can get us to whine and complain when we have little — he wins. Or, rob us of the enjoyment when God chooses to honor us with wealth — he wins again. What is the *secret* of Paul's success? Praise be to God! What cannot be accomplished in the *flesh* is done in the *Spirit*! God, through the power of His Holy Spirit can give us the strength to fight off all sin ... discontentment and condemnation. By putting in practice "right" thoughts we wrestle our minds into submission through the power of truth and scripture.

As we continue to walk with Him, the Holy Spirit fills us with His goodness and as we are filled, there is less and less room for sin. Then we will enter His gates with thanksgiving in our hearts and into his courts with praise. Fill me with Your Spirit today. I give my life to You again.

**I know what it is to be in need, and I
know what it is to have plenty.
I have learned the secret of being content in any and
Every situation, whether well fed or hungry,
Whether in plenty or in want.
I can do everything through him who gives me strength.**

Philippians 4:12&13

November 1, 2005

My heart is full of the Lord, of both His joy and the fellowship of His suffering. It is so strange walking with the Lord. How could I taste such a sweetness in Him, such satisfaction, and in the same cup heavy sorrow? I long to transcend my own wickedness. The sins that keep me from soaring in airy places, places of righteousness. Daily I struggle with the love of this world and all that it has to offer. I am a puppet with no strings. The Lord has delivered me from this world and its hold on me. He has severed the strings. So why do I stand on the stage — dance and twirl — at the puppeteer's command? It sickens me and yet there I am. Where is the victory? Is there hope? I trust the Lord for HE IS ABLE and HE WILL DO IT! Lord, You are good, only You! Thank You for giving Your goodness to me — thank You! Thank You that the gravity of that "goodness" is such, that no amount of my "badness" can tip the scales. I cling to You. The words of the old hymn, "I Need Thee Every Hour" hold my thoughts. I remind myself that I don't have to plead in desperation to have You near. By faith, I know You are with me at every moment. You don't even walk beside me — You are in me! What a mystery! Who can fathom? You God — Creator of every living thing, ruler of the universe, sovereign king, perfect in power, knowledge and love, God of Adam, Abraham, Isaac and Jacob, God of the Israelites, God of Peter, John, Mary, Paul and on through the ages. You have imparted Your Holy self to me. I am betrothed to You. Oh, how I want to be a delightful bride to You — to be a joy and not a burden! I am not a burden! I know Your love. It pours over me. It actually bubbles in me, washing me, cleansing me, from the inside out. Glory and honor to You my champion!

Heidi

The Robe

I have been lying in bed for the past hour, trying in vain to take a much-needed nap. But the wheels of my mind keep churning and will not be stopped, so I surrender to the pen. Let me give you a peek into the "goings on" of my mind.

As I lay my head on the pillow, my thoughts trail off to how serendipitous it was that I had just received a phone call from my hair salon saying due to some mishap they would need to reschedule my appointment. Normally this would be disappointing, but today it is welcome. I have been dealing with insomnia for a couple of days and woke up this morning in a terrible disposition. I got my children off to school and since it is Thursday, had the added blessing of leaving my youngest at a mother's day out program at a local church.

Nothing lightened my spirit though. My only thought was, "How am I going to make it till bedtime?" Here I was, with a golden opportunity to catch up on some desperately needed rest and instead of drifting off into peaceful slumber, I begin my journey down the familiar beaten path of self-depreciation.

"What's wrong with me?" I ask. "I am such a WEENIE!"

Images that I had seen on T.V. the past few weeks of the war in Iraq, plagued me. Those brave soldiers suffering all the discomforts of battle, such as heavy gear and chemical weapon suits in 100 degree weather. I think *I* have sleep deprivation. I can only imagine what it must be like for them, stealing a few hours of rest in the darkness. I know for a fact they aren't sleeping on plush, king-size beds with 400 count silky smooth sheets … in AIR CONDITIONING. I'm sure they have food, but nothing to what I'm accustomed to. Then there is the less than ideal hygiene and sanitation. I'm not sure I want to know how they deal with that.

Next, I start putting myself in place of an actual Iraqi family — in a war zone — possibly without electricity or running water. Nights filled with sounds of bullets and explosions, except it is no nightmare. Theirs is an insomnia birthed out of fear that their windows might be smashed in at any moment. Truthfully, even the thought is so far removed from my personal experience that it is difficult to empathize.

This line of thinking might cause some to send a prayer to heaven for these unfortunate souls, or to pray a prayer of thanksgiving for the protection, safety and freedoms we enjoy. *I* do not fall into that category. This line of thinking drives *me* to further character pummeling. Disgusted with myself, "How can I even call myself a Christian? Waa! Waa! I'm just a big baby!" My own voice taunts me.

You see, I have a self-diagnosed disability. I'll call it 100/100 vision. In the natural, I look at everything with the standard being perfect. Any deviance is just cause for chastisement. But as I age and hopefully mature (the two don't automatically go hand in hand), I am learning to put on the "glasses of grace." They help to correct my eyesight both when I look at myself and at others. This is definitely a time to put them on!

Now what do I see? God does not judge me on my ability to handle discomfort. I am not more righteous in His sight if I can endure extreme cold without a coat, or toilets in the ground with no toilet paper. I am not deemed more holy if I can walk bare-foot on hot coals or take a whip to my own back. He does not give out "A's" for eating bread without butter or pancakes without syrup. Our "holiness" or "goodness" has no correlation to our creature comforts or the lack thereof.

My grandmother once told me of the trials her ancestors endured when they settled in the Oklahoma territory. Living in sod houses, they cooked their meals over manure fires. Some found joy and kept their faith in God through hunger and hardship; others became caustic and hard, full of bitterness. I cannot judge myself on the fact that I simply don't perform well when sleep deprived. I can only look at my life and all the dirty, imperfect, smelly rags that I wear and when Jesus says, "Here! Here is a lovely, soft, white robe, without stain — put it on!" The only sane thing to do … is graciously take it. That is how I'll be judged. Am I wearing the robe or not?

All of us have become like one who is unclean,
And all our righteous acts are like filthy rags;
We all shrivel up like a leaf, and like the wind
Our sins sweep us away.
Come now, let us reason together, says the Lord.
Though your sins are like scarlet,
They shall be as white as snow;
Though they are red as crimson,
They shall be like wool.

Isaiah 64:6 & 1:18

January 8, 2004

I have been reading over my journals. My Lord and God — I am so amazed! Amazed at Your faithfulness! How on earth did our family survive such darkness? You have answered my prayers. You work miracles! You have filled so many longings of my heart! I have known such goodness. Thank You for giving me eyes to see it.

I Have Lived

I have lived life — really lived.
I have known the love of which authors and poets write — of
thunderous booms that rock the foundations under my feet.
Of cravings so sweet — and lips like magnets
— pulling me to their power.
Of breath so warm and gentle upon my neck the room would turn and
press so hard strong legs could not carry me.
I have known and been known in the mystical way that only those
who live in eternal bliss could understand — not just in flesh.
But that which is unreachable, untouchable fuses to
its immortal home where no man can separate.
I have known the comfort of being safe in arms that will not cast away.
I have been beautiful in someone's eyes.
I have known the chivalry of one brave knight who risked
himself — charging with white steed — to rescue me.
I have known the thrill of being a harbor for life.
I have watched it grow and roll my belly like an ocean tide.
I have looked into the eyes of my babe and
been everything and seen eternity.

I have known the scratchy caress of tiny fingers upon my
breast when twilight hours brought us together. Where
we were the only two people in the universe.
I have known the sweet agony of balancing my baby on one
hip until my back would ache because only I would do.
Not just once, but four times, I have had spring in my womb.
I have heard the voices of angels in music.
I have had my taste buds erupt with pleasure as the
sweet nectar of a peach crowns summer delights.
I have seen the sun rise in silence with a long straight road ahead.
I have awakened after a peaceful night's rest.
I have had my fill and more — oh yes, I have been here.

Heidi

Insect Repellent

Journals are a wonderful thing because they are a documentation of God's moving in our lives. Sometimes I too easily fall into the "stinkin' thinkin'" pit and deride myself for being a miserable excuse of a Christian, facing the same sin and weaknesses over and over again. Because we can't escape ourselves, much of the change that is taking place is so slow and steady that progress is virtually undetectable. Journaling provides some tangible source of measurement ... not just of our faithfulness but of God's.

A particular entry caught my attention—and it goes something like this:

Oh God! You are so good to me! I don't deserve such goodness, but I gratefully receive it. This morning there are voices in my head — like pesky flies buzzing by my ears. Saying things like: *Who do you think you are? Nobody, that's right. Writer's like you are a dime a dozen. Mediocrity is your middle name — no, your first name! Nothing you do has any real greatness or merit whatsoever.* Buzz...Buzz...Buzzzzzz.

THANK YOU LORD FOR INSECT REPELLENT!

Almost immediately I responded to those obnoxious pests. You're right! There isn't anything particularly extraordinary about me or what I do. I'm not brilliant, resplendent or genius. *BUT* ... my God IS! He is EXTRAORDINARY! He is RESPLENDENT! He is

GENUIS! And if *HE* chooses to bless me who can stop Him!? As long as I am seeking Him and serving Him with my whole heart, mind and strength then my life WILL achieve its purpose. I don't have to worry because HE IS FAITHFUL. As if somehow my God, the creator of the universe, full of love and compassion towards His children, could be rendered impotent! BLASPHEMOUS! He is OMNIPOTENT!

Now *that's* a good confession! There would have been a day that those voices would have sent me spiraling into defeatism. Those bugs not only would have buzzed around me but eaten me alive — injecting a paralyzing poison, making me unfit for any good work. I read this morning in Revelation 12 that the dragon, better known as Satan, was enraged at the woman and went off to make war against the rest of her offspring — those who obey God's commandments and hold to the testimony of Jesus.

Enraged. That is a pretty descriptive word. And he is at war with us …*me*! In my own personal experience the battleground lies right between my two ears. It is in my *thinking.* If Satan or his emissaries can mess with my head, they mess up my life. At one time it seemed that wicked old Devil was winning the war.

GOOD NEWS! GOOD NEWS ALERT! Back to Revelation (which can be a dizzying book, but I get the essentials) where in the end, Satan and lovers of wickedness get a dramatic dose of justice and LOSE! Jesus and partakers of His righteousness WIN!

124

So what's the secret? How am I kicking the enemy's "tushy"? Well, it all starts with belief. Not like, *I believe in you Peter Pan*. But belief that whatever God says about Himself … *IS*. So how do I know what God say's about Himself? He's telling us in every page of precious scripture, the Bible. It's in there from beginning to end. That's where He tells me that He never forsakes those who trust in Him. That He alone is faithful; that His every motive towards me, His child, is benevolent and always for good.

His desire is to bless me if only I will walk on blessable paths. His boundaries are pleasant not restrictive. Whatever we read we *must* believe! And you know what? It is amazing how much power is in just one of the above statements. If you *really* believe that every motive of your Father in heaven is for your good — just that one thing — it is amazing the "shock and awe" it wreaks on our enemy. That one idea would have kept Eve safe. She would have known that God would never keep any good thing from her.

Will I ever have something published? Will my work ever stand the test of time or make a lasting impact? Will my name ever be synonymous with those great writers … C.S. Lewis, Francine Rivers (love her!) or Jane Austin? The more I sit at the feet of Jesus, the less I care. I'm His piece of clay, His workmanship and whatever He's making, is perfect!

**For though we live in the world, we do
not wage war as the world does.
The weapons we fight with are not
the weapons of the world.
On the contrary, they have divine**

power to demolish strongholds.
We demolish arguments and every
pretension that sets itself up
Against the knowledge of God, and we take captive
every thought and make it obedient to Christ.

II Corinthians 10: 3-5

June 27, 2005

Lord, today my reading was is Job 9. Job is responding to his friend's allegations that all these things (trials/heartaches) have come upon him because of his own sin. Job replies, "How can a mortal be righteous before God?" In the same breath he cries out defending his innocence, until once again realizes even the most righteous of men cannot compare to the holiness of You. Where Job goes wrong in his portrayal of You, is his characterizing You as "mean." Boy can I relate! In my intense time of suffering, I did the exact same thing. Because You were silent — because You didn't come with relief in my own timing. Because things seemed to go from bad to worse, I questioned the truth of a "loving" creator. I don't think I ever really doubted that You were there — I only doubted that You were good. This is exactly what Job did. I find comfort in knowing my emotional battles are tied to such great men of the Bible. Another thing that stands out, and ties in so beautifully, is my New Testament passage for the day. In Luke, Jesus said to Peter that Satan had asked to "sift him like wheat" and this, in essence, is what happened to Job. Satan came to the throne and asked for free reign to persecute Job. But in both cases You had the foresight to know that your servants, Peter and Job, would come through and then on the other side be able to strengthen their brothers. Oh God of heaven — that is my prayer — that I can take all of these years of suffering and strengthen the body of Christ.

Heidi

Epilogue

Life Verse

It is *true to form,* that I am not *true to form,* when it comes to having a "life verse." You know what a life verse is. It is "I can do all things through Christ who strengthens me." It is "And we know that in all things God works for the good of those who love Him, who have been called according to His purpose" (Romans 8:28). It is — that word — that source — carrying you through life's difficulties; the word that speaks to you deeply, the scripture that finds its way into your heart over and over again. Until recently, I didn't have one. Choosing one scripture, for me, is like selecting a dessert at a Baptist potluck. I absolutely, positively cannot limit myself to just one. I had to adopt a whole chapter.

There I was sitting in my comfy glider rocker, sipping a steamy mug of java laced with my favorite flavor, crème brule, reading my daily Psalm. The system I've adopted is to read out of the Old and New Testaments, Psalms and/or Proverbs each day. This particular day, the assigned passage was Psalm 139. David's songs have been a regular part of my diet since infancy so this was familiar ground. In fact, verses thirteen and fourteen had already secured a spot in my manuscript, so you can imagine how unexpected it was when the first several lines cupped their hands around their mouths and screamed, "Heads Up!"

It was too late. The words hit me between the eyes with the force of a bowling ball. Spiritually staggering, falling to the floor, little dancing stars above my head. I know it sounds unpleasant, but it's like being knocked over with a twenty-pound bag filled with hundred dollar bills and you don't seem to mind the impact. Why the floodlights now? A superfluous question — I'm just glad the Holy Spirit flipped the switch.

This passage is a fitting closure for my book. The answers to every desperate cry to the Lord in my sad journals are met in each savory line. I challenge you to really ruminate on each phrase, allowing the flavors to explode in your spirit. I trust you, Lord, to make this a gift to all who are ready to hear, as You have so benevolently bestowed it upon me.

> **O Lord, you have searched me and you know me.**
> **You know when I sit and when I rise; you**
> **perceive my thoughts from afar.**
> **You discern my going out and my lying down;**
> **You are familiar with all my ways.**
> **Before a word is on my tongue you**
> **know it completely, O Lord.**

Growing up in a household where I was fifth of six children, I understand the "pack" mentality. Very few things were ever mine. Everything was community property. When I had my first child I secretly delighted in ordering anything monogrammed. Having *Meghan* or *Mikey* etched onto a toy or towel seemed so individual, so indulgent, so frivolous and so special! When I read this passage, I felt the God of the universe, the creator of billions of people through the ages, take the fire of the Spirit and sear my name — a name that only He knows — deep inside. Branding me with His love. His work in my life has been especially designed for me, a custom fit! Nothing is chance or coincidence. I am purposeful! I am deliberate!

He *knows* me. I cannot say for sure that this was the author's intent, but the word in Hebrew that is used in verse one is pronounced "yaw-dah" and it is the same word that is also used in the King James Version when referring to the sexual intimacy of Adam when he *knew* his wife Eve. Isn't that beautiful? What this means to me, and what resonates in my spirit, is that God is one with me. In the same secret and mystical way that two people, a man and a woman, become one flesh — so He knows me intimately. He is not just aware of my existence, He is inside of me — my thoughts. He understands the parts of me that I don't understand yet. Wow!

Michael and I are in our nineteenth year of marriage and it can get a little creepy how well we know each other — how synchronized our thoughts are. Sometimes we'll just blurt some random thing out at the same time and look at each other astonished. When we go out to eat together, I know that Michael could order for me and it would be a winner every time. He knows that I like my iced-tea unsweetened, my steak medium well to well done, and my eggs scrambled with cheese. He knows that I prefer unique hole-in-the-wall places to chains, and though hard to come by in a super-sized society — small portions. He knows when we walk into a room whether it will be stressful for me. He knows if I'm trying to hide something that is gnawing at me. He *knows* me and I imagine if we live to see thirty or forty more years together, we will reach new levels of intimacy that are presently inconceivable. As much as Michael will ever be able to know me, it is only a knock-off, a lesser replica of the oneness and intimacy that the Lord desires to experience with me and with you.

You hem me in, behind and before; you
have laid your hand upon me.
Such knowledge is too wonderful for
me, too lofty for me to attain.

I am utterly safe in the Lord's care. He won't let me go too far or lag behind. He'll push or block when necessary. Has your husband ever laid his hand in the small of your back when you were walking amidst a crowd or through a door? I love that! It is such a turn on! A small gesture of ownership and protection that communicates both to me and onlookers, *she's mine.* But it is also a gentle guiding. He is the only man that can rightfully put his hand there and lovingly direct me. That is how I visualize God — laying His hand upon me. There He is with His unseen beautiful hand, in the small of my back saying, "Let's go through this door." These kinds of thoughts are so incredible, so delightful, they truly are *too lofty to attain.*

Where can I go from your Spirit?
Where can I flee from your presence?
If I go up to the heavens, you are there;
If I make my bed in the depths, you are there.
If I rise on the wings of the dawn, if I
settle on the far side of the sea,
Even there your hand will guide me,
Your right hand will hold me fast.
If I say, "Surely the darkness will hide me
and the light become night around me,"
Even the darkness will not be dark to
You; the night will shine like the day,
For darkness is as light to You.

Wow! For someone who was diagnosed with bi-polar and experienced both soaring in the heavens and making my bed in hell, the comfort of this passage is profound! Looking back, I now see how present God was. I was never abandoned — He was with me every moment. Not only was He there — He ordained it. The scripture seems to imply divine purpose. The night was all around me and I saw no hope — only despair — still everything was as bright as day to God. There's no stubbing His toe in the dark. He knew exactly where He was going and what He was doing. He had a map — a strategy. Peace — that's what such knowledge brings.

I have had many times since when the depression rears its ugly head and tries to sink grimy fingernails into me. The sun would appear to be eclipsed. There have been horrible disappointments, betrayals and tragedies. But now I walk with so much more grace (I wish I could say *complete* grace), because whether I feel it or not, I know by faith a hand — His hand — has got a hold of me. Even if I am blind to my way, He's got His night vision goggles on.

For you created my inmost being,
You knit me together in my mother's womb.
I praise You because I am fearfully and wonderfully made;
Your works are wonderful, I know that full well.
My frame was not hidden from You when
I was made in the secret place.
When I was woven together in the depths of the earth,
Your eyes saw my unformed body.

Now — the celebration! For so many years I saw my particular wiring as defective — a disability to be tolerated and a cripple going through life who was just going to have to make the best of it. Not so! I was *created* this way — designed — not some factory defect! God deliberately fashioned me in my mother's womb to not enjoy (or at least be extremely drained) by big, loud parties. God knew that Chuck E. Cheese and Disney World visits should be few and far between. The fact that I require more sleep and quiet-time than others is precise God-wiring. I don't have to be embarrassed or guilty because I function differently. According to the psalmist we are to be terrified — in reverent awe — of how God has woven us together. God has something to reveal about Himself through me. I am an ambassador of His glory through my body and how I am made! When God looks at me and I am functioning according to His instructions He gets all tickled!

All the days ordained for me were written in Your book
Before one of them came to be.

Why should I fear death? And truthfully, I have for most of my life. God has a schedule; a well thought out beginning and an end. He is involved in every detail of me. I was born at just the right time and I will go to sleep at just the right time. It is all in His perfect care. When you are convinced of the benevolence of God — that He is supremely good — and all He does is for your good, then trusting your time frame on this earth should be a snap. If I am in relationship with the Almighty God — He knows me and I know Him — then I don't have any business fearing when I step into a plane, lay my head on my pillow at night when my husband travels, or drive across a mix master bridge in southern California. I can be at rest. He knows how long my stay needs to be and HE IS GOOD!

How precious to me are Your thoughts, O God!
How vast is the sum of them!
Were I to count them, they would
outnumber the grains of sand.
When I awake I am still with You.

To ever truly be able to enjoy this chapter and eat of its meat down to the bone, you have to have an appreciation for your own thoughts and for God's. You have to have the proper perspective of your own humanity and lowliness and of God's supreme divinity and highness. His thoughts, His ways, His decisions are so much greater, higher and more perfect than your own. And He delights to let us in on some of His secrets. But any understanding we have is what He graciously condescends to reveal to us. It was my own pride that kept me from enjoying this knowledge for so long, because somewhere deep in me I had lifted myself up to the heavens and thought God needed to explain himself — to answer to — me! The audacity!

> *If only You would slay the wicked, O God!*
> *Away from me you bloodthirsty men!*
> *They speak of You with evil intent; Your*
> *adversaries misuse Your name.*
> *Do I not hate those who hate You O Lord,*
> *and abhor those who rise against You?*
> *I have nothing but hatred for them;*
> *I count them my enemies.*

This struck me as odd at first. How does this violence fit into the greater context? Where exactly does this puzzle piece fit? Here we have all of this beautiful poetic imagery of God's great love and then all of the sudden the song turns bellicose, raging against wickedness. Hold on — emotional whiplash! As I meditated further, it came into focus and was completely rational. In my own life I have found that the more deeply God plummets the depths of my heart injecting me with His love, I get strangely more hostile. I get hostile towards perversion and the sins that have us enslaved. I look around at the infestation of wickedness and lies that pervade the world — even more disturbing, the church — and zeal consumes me.

Our precious Lord is being blasphemed! Think about how you feel when someone you love is mistreated. When a child of mine is rejected or slandered I get pretty ticked off.

One time I told my son that if he ever heard "locker room" talk about my daughter, his sister, or some boy was defaming her character, I gave him permission to knock his block off — too punch him in the nose. He said, "But mom, I would get kicked out of school." To which I replied, "Well, then I'll home school you and take you to Disneyworld." Now you may be appalled at me, but it is my conviction that there *is* appropriate violence, and today we are far too passive in matters of honor. So I completely "get" the heart of the writer who is consumed with a passion for holiness and protecting the "name" of His beloved God.

> *Search me, O God, and know my heart; test*
> *me and know my anxious thoughts.*
> *See if there is any offensive way in me,*
> *and lead me in the way everlasting.*

The Psalm has come to and end. My chapter has come to an end. And the chapter of my life where I am writing this book — has come to an end. It seems right to me to echo this prayer.

Here I am. Here is my work, Lord. I lay it at your feet. You are the author and perfector of my faith, my life, and my creations. Search me O Lord, test me and see if there is anything in me that is displeasing to you. Root it out and lead me in the way — Your good and pleasing way that leads to life everlasting.

AMEN and THE END!

Printed in the United States
145442LV00001B/1/P

9 781604 813197